The Promise

Revealing the Purpose of Your Soul

Therèse Tappouni

Synergy Books

THE PROMISE: REVEALING THE PURPOSE OF YOUR SOUL
PUBLISHED BY SYNERGY BOOKS
P.O. Box 80107
Austin, Texas 78758

For more information about our books, please write to us, call
512.478.2028, or visit our website at www.synergybooks.net.

ISBN-13: 978-1-933538-97-6
ISBN-10: 1-933538-97-X

Library of Congress Cataloging-in-Publication Data

Tappouni, Therese, 1942-
   The promise : revealing the purpose of your soul / Therese Tappouni.
      p. cm.
   ISBN-13: 978-1-933538-97-6 (hardcover : alk. paper)
   ISBN-10: 1-933538-97-X (hardcover : alk. paper)
1. Spirituality. 2. Soul. 3. Life. I. Title.
BL624.T369 2008
204--dc22

                              2007027695

10 9 8 7 6 5 4 3 2 1

Acknowledgments

To the gifted teachers and mystics Jean Houston and Peggy Rubin, who are True North and bearers of The Promise; Deepak Chopra, who made physics and mystics part of my world; Jean Shinoda Bolen, whose books opened me to the life of the Archetype; and Joan Borysenko, who never forgets that ritual and honesty are the faces of truth. To Cheryl Thomas, the most gifted of healers and sister of the soul. And, with great gratitude for his heart, Michael Hoppé, who generously allowed me to use his music on the CD.

To Michelle Tappouni, Mary Tappouni, Christopher Tappouni, Catherine Burkee, and Kathy Sessano, who read parts of this book as it developed and gave me their loving, creative feedback. My special gratitude to the entire BookPros team who saw, and brought about, my vision. I felt supported from above and below.

To Jerome, who asked me to take on this task in order that I should become that which I was meant to be.

And, as always, to my beloved family and my partner and superlative editor, Lance Ware, who make this life a joy to explore and who continue to encourage my best and truest self. Without them, this book would still be a dream.

Dedication

I dedicate this work to all the humans in this accelerated time of becoming who display courage and compassion in the face of the everyday, especially the women of my workshops who come with open hearts and great expectations and go on to do the work of their souls. I ask that this book be received as it was written: in love and prayer for the reimagining of our world.

Table of Contents

Walking in your Truth is perfection and the way of the light.
No one who walks this path is ever alone. Truth is the spark
of all essence and essence is the spark of all Truth.
The way to the Promise is by way of the Truth.

—Jerome

For how long will you continue to listen to those dark shouters,
caution and prudence?
Fall in! Fall in!

—Mary Oliver, "Have You Ever Tried to Enter the Long Black
Branches?"

Preface

This is a book about Mystery and the Sacred and our everyday lives as *humans in the process of becoming*. I have been told, in wondrous and blessed revelations, that before we take on this human life, we make a Promise. The Promise our soul makes to our Creator, and those who will guide us, is that we will do our best to discover and fulfill our individual destiny in this lifetime. This Promise, this destiny, is held in our soul as we enter our bodies. In return, we *receive* a Promise: all the tools and guidance will be revealed, as needed, once we set our foot on the path of discovery. This journey begins when we consciously reflect our truth in our inner and outer lives. Then, we remember our Promise.

Despite, and possibly because of, the uncertainty hanging over the world, we can find guidance, comfort, and individual personal truth by uncovering our deepest purpose encoded in our soul's Promise. It is my intention to assist you in uncovering and fulfilling your Promise as we travel the path together.

The phenomenal success of books about manifesting our desires speaks to the need of people to believe there is more than this physical body being born and dying in a world that is all about the material. In fact, many recent articles on research done in this area point out that people in the United States, the richest industrialized country in the world, rank 23rd in happiness. We were once number one. In *AARP The Magazine* of May/June 2007, "...according to research compiled at the

University of Leicester: Alcoholism, suicide and depression rates have soared, with fewer than one in three Americans claiming to be 'very happy.' Even more frightening is the trickle-down effect of this malaise on our kids. Studies suggest that today's average American child reports suffering higher levels of anxiety than the average child under psychiatric care in the 1950s."

Finding ways to accumulate more, resulting in children and adults with more toys, more activities, and more space per person than ever imagined, has not led to an increase in satisfaction—quite the opposite. The search for and the process of attracting what we need is as old as time. There is no secret, but we have forgotten the purpose of attraction. I see this searching and worry when it is exploited by those who simply tell you to use the miracles of your soul and the universe to get more *stuff*. We are so much more than that! Once we use our hearts, souls, and minds to uncover the Promise we made to ourselves and our creation, *then* we will know, intuitively and through the tools I share in this book, what to do with our wisdom and power to create the glorious life we were meant to have. Instant gratification is not the key, nor is focusing on the material things that we desire.

Plato said, "The learning and knowledge that we have is, at the most, but little compared with that of which we are ignorant." This is true of me, and I know that what I can teach is that which I have absolute knowing about—my own life experiences and the messages I have received from enlightened teachers. The story of each life is as individual as fingerprints, but an examined intentional life leads to the same knowledge: *what we Promised to do on this planet, what was Promised to us, and how finding our personal Truth will show us both of these things.*

I knew when my life was about to shift into a new reality. Magic and movement were in the air and there was no stopping them. Multiple messages, and messengers, told me to tell "The Truth" and reveal "The Promise." This book traces how I did precisely that, in the belief that the template of my journey will help others to map and recognize their own journey. We are meant for truth telling—truth with a capital *T*. The promises given to us throughout history—from prophets, saints, writers, poets, musicians, artists, and happenings in our own lives—can only be revealed by telling our Truth. In every part of this book, you will hear that message from many sources, including those that prompt us by way of our internal knowing. It is the one thing to take with you, body and spirit, to give birth to the rest of your life.

The truth is that despite changes in our lives, only one thing remains constant, and that is love. The soul is pure love and a container for our purpose and destiny. It resides in this wonderful body that experiences everything: pain, joy, ecstasy, and sorrow. When we are not in the service of love, which is often because we are also human, we feel its loss in our bodies and spirits. This is an elegant warning system; a gift of the Universe. The body speaks to us through our emotions so we can understand. The soul itself *never* changes, but as we seek our truth, our understanding of our soul changes. The soul came *with* us, *in* us, *is* us, at birth. It stays with us during our life, prompting us to be all that we can be, and goes on *as* us after death. This is a Promise. We do not die. We may die to our bodies, but that is insignificant in the vastness of time and the significance of our soul's work. My soul tells me I will have to tell *my* Truth—all of it. It is a choice I do not make lightly, but I make it in the knowledge that Truth is love and my soul wants me to be love.

Again, it is my intention, through this work, to assist you in uncovering and fulfilling your own personal Promise through revealing the Truth of your life. Then, you will be living the life designed by your soul.

The following story began my journey into the writing of this book.

It is a soft, flower-scented January evening in Florida. The year 2002 lies ahead of us, an empty path of possibility. Six women gather for a healing meditation in the home of Jill McCann, a gifted therapist and light-worker in St. Petersburg. I am suffering from chronic pain that overlays every atom of my daily life. I want help. I seek healing. I've been told about Jill's work and have resisted letting go of my earthbound self to trust my spirit to go where it needs to. The pain has driven me here.

Music floats into the room as we all close our eyes and Jill's quiet voice leads us into our meditation. She does work that is unfamiliar to me in this life, but familiar somehow in my soul. I promise myself to go with her guid-

ance, no matter where it leads. I am in total trust bred from total desperation. We are creating a pyramid of light around ourselves, absorbing light into our bodies, and eventually, sending it out to the entire planet.

Jill asks us to enter the sacred pyramid, which is the fifth dimension or higher—she calls this the Christ consciousness, our higher self. I see the pyramid clearly above me. The capstone is filled with an undulating rainbow; a crystal projects up and down, the down pointing above a crystal table. I am lying, somehow, on the table. Surprisingly, the material that looks like crystal fits like a soft mold around my body, changing into a reclining chair. It is so comfortable! Vibrant pink and purple flow from the material through my body, and I see an angel at my head and feet, vibrating silver and purple sound-light. I am enveloped from below by a purple flame, energetic but not hot. I feel as if I'm being cleansed. I hear that my energy and higher purpose for the year is love and kindness, represented by purple and rose vibrations.

The air in the room is charged, the roof disappears; the heavens are chiming with blessings. I hear a voice saying:

"I've been waiting for you since you were a child."

*I see him as he comes near. He is wearing a hooded robe, his gentle, intelligent eyes compassionate in the shadows. He holds up a book. I can see green, maybe velvet, but it is covered with mist, and I can't read the title. He brings me closer, and I see the cover—***The Promise***. The book is decorated with gold markings. "Be gentle, be loving. Teach! Tell about the Truth and The Promise." And he is gone.*

Part One:

THE JOURNEY

*If you do not tell the truth about yourself,
you cannot tell it about other people.*

—Virginia Woolf

In My New Beginning

In the mid-1990s, after thirty-five years of marriage, my husband and I divorced. The children had grown, I was over fifty, and I was being asked to re-birth myself; but as what was in question. I had never stopped writing, even while raising my six children, but a short attention span resulting from stress had me limited to writing haiku. I knew I had been given a gift and a directive by my soul, but I was wandering in the wilderness. In ancient times, an elder knew their place—a place of wisdom from which the young could learn. It is not like that anymore. People over fifty, especially women, have lost their place of honor. I needed to invent such a space to fit myself and the woman I was becoming. It was in this time of struggle that I wrote **Grief Storm**.

Grief Storm

It came up like a brief shower,
smelling of fresh grass, showing
only a small ribbon of black as it
edged over mother mountain.
But, in a chill buried beneath
my rib cage, I knew it was
coming for me, sensed there was
no safety, not even in the
farthest cobwebs of the cellar.

Time to inhale thunder, risk
my eyes to the jagged fire
of lightning. I put on a gown
red as birthing blood, let down
my hair. It rises, fine wire
to test the air, fans around my
face, copper antennae daring
nature's animal power to
approach me. There is no time
like the past to lead me to my
future. I lay on wet grass under
our ancient oak, aware of warnings
about trees and lightning:
but I know this one is my
protector. I watch old
beliefs lift from my belly,
church fathers naked, vestments
sacrificed to the truth about
men and women. Years of marriage
sift from my cells, their smoke rising
from breasts and loins. Hot tears
flow, mountain torrents after
snow melt: sorrow bathes women
cast aside, treated as less because
they spoke Truth, healed freely,
used the gifts they had been given;
fountains of grief for all the girl
children left to die or cut away
from their feminine knowing.
Flood waters rise beneath my hips,
float me to the stream, river
and bay until I reach the ocean
of Baptism, rest on the salt

of forgiveness. I watch dark
clouds of regret escape across
the sun, burst into red-gold
promises of possibilities.
Waves lap against the soles
of my feet, edge me back
to dry land where I find myself
lying in that same grass near the
same house and tree, steam
rising from my head as incense.

Can you feel the change in the air—spirit, soul, and the word "Truth" arising like incense? I was receiving the messages I would need in a form that made sense to me. That's where I was in 1998, two years after I began living alone, on a Sunday afternoon that created an abrupt turn in my path. A friend who could not drive asked me to take her to an Alan Cohen lecture at a local Unity church. I enjoyed Alan's talk, which he closed with the following words: "If you truly want to know who you are and what you are meant to do on this planet, join me in Maui." The light in the church became soft and golden. Chills ran up and down my arms, lifting the hair on my head. These shivery sensations and the light are signs from our spirits to our bodies that something is going on. I had never traveled a long distance alone, and I had never been to Hawaii. I took Alan's brochure and slept with it under my pillow. The money that was meant to go in my retirement account began to look like travel funds as I dreamed the smell of frangipani. Despite my conservative nature and my fear around money, I traveled to Maui in April of 1998. There, a new life began for me as surely as BC is separate from AD.

After the heart-opening workshop with Alan, I stayed on for three days, descending and ascending into the ancient wisdom of Maui, writing constantly. During Alan's workshop, we were given a fifteen-minute glimpse into the three-hour mystery of Hawaiian Temple massage. Two beautiful people, a man and woman, recreated the ancient art in front of our eyes. Though the music and ritual were profoundly moving, I didn't sign up. I was afraid of what might happen if I surrendered my body to their touch. Even after all the work, I was still in a place of fear.

The day I was leaving Alan's workshop, in the parking lot, I saw the two people who had demonstrated the massage. An unseen hand pushed against my back, and I found myself walking up to Tom and Jodi, asking if they had an appointment available the next day. They had just gotten a cancellation and agreed to pick me up the next afternoon. As I walked to the car, my inner doubting voice began throwing up objections: "You've spent enough money. You need to spend your remaining time writing. You don't know these people."

I was still so resistant to letting go of control and allowing my inner story to reveal itself. Like taking the stopper out of the genie's bottle, I would have to deal with whatever appeared.

What would happen if one woman told the truth about her life? The world would split open.

—Murial Ruckeyser, poet

The Temple

Tom picks me up at my Bed and Breakfast. I have fasted, showered, meditated, removed my contacts and jewelry, washed my face clean of any makeup, and am wearing a long, loose gown. Like Inanna before me, I am stripped of all artifice. He drives me up into the hills, asking me along the way about my life and why I'm here. It is a long, breathtaking drive. Jodi waits at the door of a small house. It is a Temple, complete with silk hangings, candles, and a pristine sheeted table facing nothing but the mountain and a sweep down to the ocean. It is dark when we begin to talk, and both of them lovingly draw from me my intentions and my fears: my fears of not being able to release my ex-husband; a lousy body image coming from the divorce and earlier rejection; being drawn back into the drama awaiting me at home around support and money; and not doing my work. So many fears! I see the moon rise as I talk.

They are warmth and loving kindness incarnate as they tell me their training instructs them to look at the human body as a temple for the spirit, not as the world judges a body. At its best, the massage will reveal to me the purpose of my life while releasing past trauma. At the least, I will be totally relaxed. They leave me to undress. I lie facedown on the table, pull a crisp clean white sheet up over my naked body. They return and the room is filled with a Hawaiian chant issuing from hidden speakers. It is an ancient voice, female, rich and dark with wisdom. I turn my head to the side and they are standing with feet planted, knees bent, and arms weaving ritual above my body. Time retreats and the moon outlines the set of their bodies, the rootedness of their feet and legs. They are part of a long line of healers and shamans, known as Kahuna in this mystical land, and I am about to be birthed into their presence.

I turn my face back into the table and I hear their powerful breathing. There is a quick inhale, as if breath is pulled through a hollow tube—a sipping sound—and then a full warm exhale of air against my back. Their hands come to rest firmly on my spine and legs; I pay attention to my breathing. The music, the breeze, the scents of frangipani and pine, the sound of the old woman's voice: it is all so familiar. I hear myself speak. My voice whispers into the fragrant room, settles softly into my ears:

"Yes, Grandmother, I know you…"

Scented oil is stroked lavishly on my body. I enter a movie, falling back in time. I see me, but another me. I am wearing a long white gown, a wreath of orchids on my head, and my arms are full of fragrant flowers. There is a steady cadence of drums. I sit on a beautiful bench, laying the flowers beside me, and I see that I am facing a large pyramid with steps going around. At the top of the steps stands a man. He comes down toward me, and I recognize him as my ex-husband. I stand and offer him the flowers. He turns his back and walks away toward the mountains.

Again, a man appears on the stairs and comes toward me. He is blond and is wearing a crown of shiny dark leaves. I think I am to offer him the flowers, but he stops and looks toward the forest. I hear a wailing coming from the trees and know it is the sound of a beast. I am not afraid. I go toward the trees, alone, and a man/beast comes toward me, growling and fierce—like the Ben Gunn character in Treasure Island. I sit down in front of him and raise my flowers in my arms. Tears flow down his cheeks and into his beard as he takes the flowers from me. Slowly, he turns and goes back into the forest. I return to the pyramid and the blond man comes to me and takes my hands.

I am back in the room, but I am still partially in the movie of my unconscious. The music has changed. It is more primitive, more movement based. Tom and Jodi are leaning over and on my body using forearms and elbows. I am still on my stomach, my eyes in darkness. The only pain I feel is in my back, but I am crying. I see my ex-husband disappearing, a tiny figure moving off into the distance. I become more aware of the physical part of the massage, yet see myself being laid on a marble table in preparation for a ceremony—I think it is to be my wedding. An old woman with long dark braids, and an orchid behind her ear, is attending me. I feel safe in her presence.

I'm back in the room as arms slide under me and glide across my abdomen and belly, and my muscles tense. I hear the instruction to breathe, and relax into my breath. The music is so familiar, so beloved.

My arms and legs are raised and lowered, bent into fluid shapes I have not experienced in years. I feel elbows and arm bones sliding alongside my bones. The pressure is deep and I border on discomfort, but I breathe into it and relax. My arms and legs are now jelly-like as they are lifted, bent, and rotated. I can't feel all of my body, but I'm fully in the massage and out of the movie. I'm being turned over without my cooperation, and though it seems to be effortless, I am fearful. Hands are manipulating my neck, and my head lolls like a flower on a stem. Now thumbs are moving up my shins in a deep ridge; pain, but it disappears.

Hands are at my throat and then descend to my breastbone. I feel pain in my left breast. I know there is no reason for this—a recent mammogram has shown nothing after more than a year of dark shadows. Aaaah—pressure on my heart chakra area and something cuts loose, drifts from me up into the sky. A wailing comes from a corner of the room. Who or what is it? And then I recognize the voice. It is mine. Arms slide around my back and arch me up, the back of my head brushes the table, and I am Jesus in the Pieta, my mother holding me. The wails turn to a soft crying.

I am walking down the aisle on my wedding day—more tears flow. Is there no end to these tears? I am rocked as hands stroke my abdomen, then four arms are under and over and I am being rocked from side to side. I see my womb, watch as my babies arrive, one after the other. Again, the hands are pressing on the bones just above my breasts, and I don't think I can take any more. I cry out in hurt, grief, sadness—HUGE sadness. Relief, instant, as each of my adult children appears beside the table. "I love you, Mom." My ex-husband is standing at the head of the table. "I loved you the best I knew how, you know." He walks away but everyone else stays. I am filled with peace; the hands on me are warm and comforting. My cells have yielded up the past and I am new.

Hands are stroking my face, my eyes, even my ears. Someone cradles my head. I am in pure bliss. My family is gone—I didn't see them leave—but they will always be with me. My limbs are arranged; they have no mind of their own. Tom and Jodi lift the sheet, floating it above me, the way we did as children, or when making the bed, then draw it from my toes up over my

9

head, the sheet touching my body lightly as it goes, exposing my toes first, and my head last. They have done this now three times, breathing on the sheet each time. Throughout, they have blown away the things that surface from my body. Each part of me that is revealed as they slide the sheet up is a new me being born. They cover me and leave me to rest.

I don't know how much time has passed, but they have returned to the room and are gently rubbing the oil from my body with a rough cotton towel. They offer me water. I feel absolutely safe and loved and born anew. This is a gift beyond price, and one I know I will carry forever. Tom tells me that the Hawaiian music they began with was for them, to call on their skills and their guides. They would usually change the music to something more appropriate for the client. In this case, they felt my body responding to the ancient music, heard my response to Grandmother, and left the music. How was it possible that I had been here for three hours? Time paused between then and now. I rest, then go into the bathroom and see my face in the mirror. I am unlined, clear, my eyes large black pools looking back at me from a great distance. I see my awakened self, rising through the darkness.

❧

The time will come
When, with elation,
You will greet yourself arriving
At your own door, in your own mirror,
And each will smile at the other's welcome,
And say, sit here, Eat.

—Derek Walcott, "Love after Love"

❧

I have met myself in the mirror. Sometimes, it is long after an experience before its lessons are fully realized in the body. In this case, the work was done directly on and in my cell structure, and there would be no return to what I knew as normal. I call on this memory whenever I need strength in the world for my work, and I hear again the voice of Grandmother. I am never without guidance.

A day earlier, on another part of the island, our group had hiked through an amazing bamboo forest, always headed toward the sound of falling water. A breathtaking view greeted me as I broke through into a glade of indescribable beauty. In the midst of grass, boulders, and flowers, a pool shimmered, formed from the tumbling waterfall above. I can still feel the sharp rocks under my feet, the cold water soothing my hot body, and the total serenity of my spirit as I dove under the thundering waterfall and floated out into the pool, the women of my group waiting for me. This memory has become part of my arsenal for returning to peace when I am in a place of turmoil. Tom, Jodi, four special women, and Grandmother are now part of my spiritual family.

My ex-husband gave me the impetus to go to Maui. I thank him for that. Part of telling the truth is acknowledging that we both danced the dance that led to the end of our marriage and allowed the beginning of new lives. However, and this is a very large however, when you begin to do forgiveness work, you *must* acknowledge your emotions. The Truth is not negated by logic. "I thank him for that," came after a lot of effort spent facing resentment, anguish, hurt, and great damage to my self-esteem.

I remember particularly one day when I was told my former husband was engaged to be married. I felt, literally, struck down. That *was* me, on the floor in my daughter's living room, on my knees. I think I was more shocked at my reaction than I was at the news. How had I wrapped up all that had been happening and stored it away? Up until then, you never would have known my life was not in perfect balance.

The next morning, against the better and wiser advice of my daughter, I got in my car and drove twelve hours straight to the mountains of North Carolina, a place where I had always been renewed. I really believed I would die in that car, the emotional pain was so overwhelming—and for twelve hours, there was no escape from my swirling thoughts and breaking heart.

The vision I had in Maui of presenting myself as a gift to my husband, who walked away, and the fearful howler in the woods, who took my gift and cried, began to make sense. I had a lot of pain and truth to face before I was ready to be a gift to anyone, including myself. The Ben Gunn character was me, howling in the woods, needing my own attention. Within these revelations were all of the elements of major drama: anger, betrayal, righteousness.

11

It was only right that I went to the mountains alone. We've been told throughout history that the journey within begins in the desert or the mountains, representing isolation. From Inanna, Persephone, Mohammed, and Jesus to the mystics and Nelson Mandela, we go alone to uncover ourselves. I didn't have forty days and forty nights, but after a week of meditation, prayer, and agonizing introspection, I started to notice the soft, pine-scented air. I was ready to *begin* the process of forgiveness and open myself to healing.

Removing the blamed one leaves a vacuum. How to dance life without a partner? I was learning that my partner was myself: my life and my growth. Other partners were being introduced to me by way of dream and meditation. I wrote the book *Walking Your Walk: A Woman's Guide to a Spirit Filled Life,* and began helping gatherings of women to see their life as a spiritual path. In 1998 I met the blond man on the stairs, and we have been together ever since. That is a story for later. He has encouraged me to write this book and tell my truth.

Earlier books cover much of my spiritual work, but leave out those things I felt were too personal or revealed too much of my inner spiritual journey. The challenge of this book was that I would "tell the Truth and realize the Promise." That meant, and I was assured of this over and over, the *whole truth*. The truth is I was intimidated by the challenge. I have received a promise that revealing the Truth is a freedom, not a fear. It's not that I don't tell the truth in my everyday life. However, I'm aware that, in order to tell the truth about other things, I must first reveal the whole truth about myself—then The Promise will be revealed. Only by demonstrating my own path to The Promise can I unearth the clues that will help others to see their lives as a journey through Truth to their destiny.

Most of life is spent growing new personalities, covering up personalities, and creating stories about ourselves that instill comfort in those who are paying attention, and in ourselves. The energy used in this process could power the sun. Those who have chosen to show their true selves are usually labeled eccentric in the least and psychotic on the far side. Some hide out in the arts, where behavior of all kinds is excused on the basis of creativity. In the sciences, the costume of genius gives one a pass. For the rest of us, it is a fear instilled by the "what will people think" mind-set.

Excavating layers of these stories to reveal the original template we were born with requires an energetic commitment equal to the original cover-up. The good news is that we are up to the task. We are, in fact, created for it. That is one large part of the Truth, and The Truth is the portal to The Promise. I invite you to risk entering here with me. Your own personal Maui experience can be recognized as the event that set you on the search for the Grail of yourself. Look for the stories in your life that led you, inexorably, to the Truth of who you are and who you are meant to be. I will feel a blessing from your companionship, and gratitude for your curiosity and courage.

Between living and dreaming there is a third thing.
Guess it.

—Antonio Machado

What I Know of Truth

Guess it! It is more than a guess. It is a feeling, a sensing in your intuitive body that can be trained. The truth can be different things at different times, but some truths are familiar, found in the same place. The unmistakable warmth of right-being can be enjoyed by going to a place we know intimately within ourselves, such as my Maui waterfall or my children. Going there evokes comfort and love. On the other hand, emotional pain touches us and we feel it in the physical body—for me, it is in the belly or the heart—and we know the truth of the pain. Those who do not love us, or love us only through their wounding, know how to find that place whenever it suits them. We vibrate to the tune of our world, and it is a tune of our own creation.

It came to me one day that **the body is the tuning fork for the Universe.** This felt like a capital T Truth. We are vibrating to the strings of truth or lack of truth entering our bodies from the outside. Sometimes truth needs a helper, like a haven in nature or in our inner life, that evokes a world outside of our experience; that place we call the mystical. Most importantly, the Truth is found only where the real I resides, and there is no mistaking it. We are home. Telling it is a matter of divesting ourselves of the layers of other personas and trusting that our true being, and the Truth, will arrive together. So, I begin with my earliest memories of what was true for me.

In the Beginning

◦◦◦

When I was a child, I caught a fleeting glimpse,
out of the corner of my eye.
I turned to look but it was gone,
I cannot put my finger on it now…

—Pink Floyd, "Comfortably Numb," lyrics by David Gilmour

◦◦◦

This song didn't become an anthem without thousands of people saying, "That's me. I know *something* was there, I was so close!"

The real question is: where is it now? It is our true essence, our true self, our true understanding of our world. It has been lost under the noise and activity around us. We must be still to find the truth. From the time I was a very small child, I had an overwhelming need for solitude. Whether I found it under the dining room table laid with a linen cloth or the back of a closet, this need was a driving force. Until I was eleven, the formal dining room of the elegant white house on South Fourth Street in Springfield, Illinois, served as the perfect hideout. Since I was not allowed to serve on the altar at Blessed Sacrament, like my brothers would be, I found an alternative. Every May during the month of the Blessed Mother, I created my own altar in the bedroom I shared with my sister, Mary. Even today, the perfumes of lilac and peony send me to a sacred place. I have had altars of my own making in my life ever since.

15

When I needed a companion, my buddy David, who lived next door, was more than happy to join me in the loft over the garage to look at old National Geographic magazines; or I would pay him a penny to watch his movies, beamed on a sheet hung on the dining room wall. His aunt Alice made us popcorn at no charge. I could handle certain humans one-on-one.

More times than I can count, I was dragged forth to participate in doings or activities arranged for me by my concerned parents. "What do you mean, you don't want to go to Jane's party? Of *course* you do. There will be lots of kids your age there." Oh, those magic, fearful words! They could bring on an instant stomach pain that was achingly real. Doctors diagnosed allergies, asthma, or, worst of all, psychological problems that required even more input from the parents. No matter the remedy, I was still drawn to time alone with my books, altar, and drawing pads in lieu of kids my own age. The Truth was that I needed that time with my soul as much as some people needed the companionship of others. This isn't fully true for everyone, but true to different degrees for anyone who would look from the corner of their eye and see the mystical reality of the world.

That is still part of my Truth today, a part I cherish in my busy life. This doesn't negate the very real delight I take in my relationships with part-ner, children, friends, and grandchildren. But make no mistake. When we are aware of the Inner Light that illumines what is true for us, we have only one choice. Follow where it shines.

A serious and devout Catholic, I was particularly devoted to the Blessed Mother. The hymns we sang during the month dedicated to her, the month of May, were hymns to the goddess in all her glory. "Oh, Mary, we crown thee with blossoms today, Queen of the Angels, Queen of the May." From the day I wore my bridal white, including veil, to pledge myself on my First Communion, I was enraptured by the ritual and beauty of this worship. I've written many poems on the subject.

May Music

On this day, oh beautiful Mother,
on this day, we give thee our love.
Near thee, Madonna, fondly we hover,

trusting thy gentle care to prove.
—Traditional Catholic hymn to Mary

Making the invisible visible, we sang
our longing for the goddess as if we
lived in Athens, Rome, or Babylon
and were about to enter the temple,
light the sacred lamps. We wore crowns
of flowers, carried clouds of peonies,
irises, and lilies of the valley to her grotto
just left of the altar, behind a gold gate.
"Near thee, Madonna," we sang, our sweet
young soprano voices rising to the domed
ceiling. I knelt to worship at her flower-
covered feet, not connecting the smiling
infant in her arms to the bleeding, agonized
man nailed above the sanctum sanctorum.
I knelt to honor the religion of my mothers.

At the beautiful, tender, lustful age of thirteen, I went to spend a weekend at the convent. My Ursuline teachers were surely aware of the heat we were experiencing as puberty flooded the cells of our bodies—they may have taken vows, but they were still women. Besides, there was always a possibility that a Mechtild, a Julian of Norwich, or a St. Teresa praising God would emerge from the fires of girlhood in lieu of Elvis worship. Anything was possible. Some early warning system had advised me that a spiritual path could be managed more easily with a cell of my own and a space of silence for prayer and meditation, and as the number of my siblings increased, so did my need.

Despite my efforts, and the hospitality of the nuns, on the third day, after the sixth Mass, I knew the convent was not my journey in life. My spiritual path lay through home, family, children, and work in the world—the least contemplative choice for a woman with a contemplative nature. I returned to my virgin bedroom determined to have both worlds: the heat that drew me to a certain boy in school and the desire that drew me to my journal, my altar, and my solitude.

I would say that I chose to have a different life. Those who believe in many incarnations would say, and have said, that I contracted to experience a life that I had not necessarily experienced before. Whatever the truth, I entered my twenties as a married woman with a child and would give birth to five more children before I was thirty. It was a vocation that felt as true and guided as anything I have ever done, and my adult children are a joy in my life. I know with my whole heart and soul that their father and I came together to bring them to this planet and to experience the creation of family from the strengths and beliefs of two totally different worlds. We were successful in that, and will be bound together in that knowledge to the end of our lives. *We also gifted the planet with human beings of great compassion and potential for this difficult time.*

Before my children reached the age where they were in school full time, I worked part-time through small, home-based businesses that were more about my self-esteem than money. In this time that saw the rise of another wave of feminism misrepresented by "You're just a *housewife?*" I baked cakes for neighborhood birthdays, sewed clothes, crafted macramé hangers for which my daughter Michelle created pots and beads, and wrote for a sports magazine. My children remember months of dodging macramé artwork in all stages of production hanging from nails in doorways.

My one stab at *real work* during the sixties was as a part-time employee for the IRS. Once we figured out what I was earning versus what I was spending to go to work, and one of my children said the baby sitter made him use a tree for a bathroom, my six-week career ended. One thing has always remained constant; I never stopped reading, writing, and going to school.

To women of *any* age, I say be courageous and follow your own intuition, the promptings of your soul. Due to my circumstances and my intuition, I rejected the formal education path. There were so many things I knew I needed to know to write and teach what my soul was telling me to write and teach. It was not a time when universities were happy to tailor a course of self-directed study, but I was determined. I went to the local universities and junior/community colleges, met with guidance counselors, and arranged to take for credit, or to audit, those courses that were part of my life design. I attended junior college two nights a week while the kids were young, feeding them supper, bathing the youngest, and fleeing out the door as their father and my oldest daughter took over bedtime duties.

When I was pregnant, I took child development and psychology courses, dovetailing my wants and my needs. I was fortunate to have a professor who was a working psychologist and allowed me to meet with him after class about my real-life issues around children and family. I have undying gratitude to the generous Dr. Gadarian for his patience and intelligence, realizing years later that I had been receiving free counseling. My sociology courses allowed the school district to appoint me as a school-community coordinator for a federal program, even though I didn't have formal credentials.

At various schools in the area I was allowed to audit Philosophy and Women's Studies courses for seniors and graduate students and then to take the graduate courses in writing. I was led through the dissertation process by a wonderful mentor as I began my first novel. And still, I had no coherent degree or graduation plan. I realize now that these angels of mercy had to do a lot of pleading and bargaining in their departments to allow what I was doing.

I have never been without guidance. I studied with master teachers like Jim McKinley, Conger Beasley, and Dan Jaffe of the University of Missouri, Kansas City; the astonishing Miller Williams of the University of Arkansas; and the wonderful poet and mentor Peter Meinke at Eckerd College in St. Petersburg, among many others. Outside of the university, Dr. Jean Houston and Peg Rubin have been the epitome of what teachers can be. Education is derived from the Latin word *educare*, "to draw out." These teachers drew out of me the best I had to offer. I am forever grateful.

I savored adult education courses for thirty years, even when I was working full time after all the children were in school. It's a wonder my brain didn't blow a fuse as I attended *Tax Laws for the Small Business* at the SBA office in Tampa (for our business. I can't say I savored that one); *Literature of the Twentieth Century* at the University of South

Florida (for my heart); and *Stress Reduction for the Over Extended* at the local Jewish Community Center (for my nerves). None of this resulted in a viable degree—my 200 plus credits have no coherence as far as the degree path is concerned. However, I am still educating myself in the same way. Wonderful teachers recommended books. I can't even imagine how many I've read. These led me to new teachers like Deepak Chopra, Joan Borysenko, and Jean Houston many years later.

Whatever happens, continue to choose what supports you. In my case, it was educating myself and satisfying my curiosity about how the body, mind, and spirit work in this world. The fact that I was able to coordinate this education with my paths in life is the greatest gift of being *choice educated*. Today, this is easier due to the proliferation of schools that recognize we are not all the same. However, it is still hard to find exactly what you are drawn to. Be persistent; you are putting together a life of meaning. It is worth the effort and the courage to ignore those who say you'll never make it without the standard diplomas. I was not aware, early on, that my studies would turn in the direction of the soul. This knowing didn't come until Maui. Simply following the thread that weaves your life is your whole (holy) path.

After my divorce, I still worked in the family business and was in daily contact with children, friends, and my ex. My journals of that time reflect a sense of certainty that *now*, at the age of fifty-five, the possibility of a room of one's own and a full-time writing life was achievable. I put the visualization with the blond man into a logical place where he *represented* something. A friend of mine had a dream of a man hovering around me. She said he was blond, of slender build, and lived near boats. I flippantly told her that *if,* and that was a *big if,* I ever opened myself to another relationship, the man would be a big bear of a man who would make me experience the feeling of being petite. If not, it would happen in my next life. I should know better than to challenge the Universal Plan!

Soon, I was contemplating a move to a quiet village on the Gulf Coast of Florida into a house of my own. I was on the third visit to this cottage, ready to sign the papers, when a phone call from a friend alerted me to the presence of a man she'd met at a Barbara Marx Hubbard conference. She gave him my phone number after he talked about the kind of spiritual relationship he desired. I protested again that I wasn't ready to even consider a mate in my life. Fresh from divorce, moving rapidly toward my life of solitude, I did not see the great movement in the spirit world that signaled the coming of my life mate and the new challenge: to build a spiritual relationship within the desires of my own life. Over the years this has become the lesson that informs my teaching.

Lance and I met on August 7, 1998. He is blond, slender, and was living at a marina. We have been together since the day we met. Our challenges and lessons are many, but I have a knowing in my heart and soul, reinforced through the messages I receive constantly from my spirit, that this is to be the second half of my life. To find our own paths and the path we are to walk together has been our work, our challenge, and our joy. There must be a complete you, a complete me, and a cooperative and loving us. The contemplative life takes place in the *me* and also in the *us*, as we learn to anchor each day in meditation and purpose. Resolving issues by bypassing the ego allows us to be in trust. There is no winner and loser—only the highest good we can discern for both of us. This is our ideal, one we sometimes fail to live up to since we are human.

I wrote the following poem many years ago concerning a friend who was medicating himself to death. It is true of many relationships. The "little pills" can be anything from excessive television watching to alcohol to hobbies that get out of hand. This wise observation of the poet John Keats is true of all our relationships:

> "I know nothing but the holiness of the heart's
> Affections and the Truth of the Imagination."

Visionary

The heart sees; it is not blind.
Society does not see; it is blind
to what matters—the *how* of you.
But my heart does see and what
it views is the true heart of you,
loving, frightened, longing,

21

home-sick. The eye of the heart is
sacred, seeing Truth where the ego
finds need for improvement. Don't
take your little pills. Let me see you
in all of your terrible beauty. And
then, if you will, see me with
the compassionate eyes of your heart.

Hidden from Sight

◦◦◦

The familiar life horizon has been outgrown: the old concepts, ideals, and emotional patterns no longer fit; the time for the passing of a threshold is at hand.

—Joseph Campbell, *The Hero with a Thousand Faces*

◦◦◦

In the hero or heroine's journey, the search for the Grail of oneself, a time will always arrive when you know you cannot go back. Back means comfort and death—death of what Jean Houston calls the *possible self*. Forward means life, albeit a new life that will not feel very comfortable at first. You must have faith in your path and your intuition.

There are many stories of the hero/heroine being stripped naked and sent into the underworld or on a dangerous quest. These are allegories about losing all the symbols and material possessions of this life in order to discover and put on the symbols and possessions of the new life. Many books exist that talk about this process, the most famous written by Joseph Campbell, but there are others (See Appendix II and III). The old myths and stories are strong guidance for the mythic hero. For those of you who are movie buffs, in *The Last Crusade*, Indiana Jones shows his hard-won faith in the quest when he steps out into the void, trusting he will be supported.

My own personal quest has been private and hidden from the everyday world. I cannot tell my truth without revealing parts of my journey.

There exists within me a life that has remained hidden until now; my sixty-third year, the end of my ninth cycle of seven. The pull of this journey, this quest for the Grail of myself, became irresistibly powerful as I approached fifty. It was my turn to step out into what appeared to be, but was not, thin air. This is a magical time. The mystical sense of difference that required solitude has erupted into serial synchronicities. Teachers are coming forward. Urgency overlays my daily life, pushing me to complete old work so I can begin anew. Mystical writers have called this "the hounds of heaven nipping at your heels."

I have managed, thus far, to be normal, maternal, nurturing, and supportive without revealing and acknowledging the visitations and miracles of my private life. There are a few glorious humans that I have trusted with my inner life, but they are rare. That time is past. If I am to share the message, I must reveal the methods and appearances of the messengers. I have experienced the whispers that follow those who are different, and I have created a persona—a *real* persona—that acknowledges little of the depths experienced when one lives a complete life. Trust yourself. Take my hand and we'll step off the cliff together.

My journey into the unknown as known began many years ago, but was nurtured in the mountains of North Carolina. On my yearly trips there, I read, studied, meditated, and connected with the mother mountain nature as I did nowhere else. After Maui, I began to enjoy massage when I went to the mountains. On this particular day, my massage therapist was on vacation. A Native American man filled in for her. The music he chose was flute and drum, very appropriate to these Cherokee-haunted mountains.

As I drifted into my usual relaxed state, I felt the presence of four bears, one at each corner of the table. They were brown bears, large and fierce yet protective of me. As I headed for sleep, my logical brain noted that there were only black bears in these mountains. The flow of energy in my body increased to a buzzing just this side of discomfort.

And then I left the table. The bears surrounded me as we climbed one of the beautiful sloped mountains so familiar and so loved. When we got to the top, they sat, creating a four square space for me. I sat facing east and saw the whole beautiful blue-green valley spread out in front of me. We were above

24

the haze that gives the Smoky Mountains their name, seeing the valley below through a misted Monet wash. My body felt so serene, so protected, and unbelievably blessed to be there. I asked for words to explain what they were showing me, and all I heard was that I was protected by the Mother and should not fear. Being in that most beautiful of natural settings made it impossible to deny the Creator's hand in my life plan.

They showed me myself as a bear, burdened with bags of "stuff" as I climbed the mountain. I was clawing at the rocky ledges, trying to get to the top. On my back were duffel bags that looked like they were filled with rocks, but I knew they represented my material concerns. As I watched, the bear that was me dropped all the bags down the side of the mountain where they disappeared into a gorge. Before I knew it, she/I was at the top. I woke up to the music of the Cherokee and the smiling face of my guide.

The Last Eight Years

∞

The Holy Spirit is our harpist,
And all strings Which are touched in Love Must sound.

—Mechtild of Magdeburg, mystic, Saxon (ca. 1207-1282)

∞

All strings! If you are loved, you will be loved as a complete instrument. If you are not loved as yourself, you are looking in the wrong places. The revving up of my personal mystical life began with Maui. I was a finely tuned instrument, waiting for the next player. Months later, the first weekend that I met Lance, I was aware that another virtuoso had arrived. Those of you who are in touch with the profound miracle of sharing your life with a mate of the soul know the state I was in when I first met the blond man from my dreams. I had been broken open so that love could enter. While I was still in that ecstatic state of arrival, another miracle occurred.

I have known Lance less than a month, and we are in his church, where he's promised to sit for a half hour in meditation on The World Day of Prayer. As we sit with our eyes closed, I feel movement coming from the altar. I can't open my eyes, but I see the imprint of a Christ figure behind my lids. He's luminous, but solid, and moving slowly toward me. My body is heating up from the luminous light surrounding him. He is now standing directly in front of

26

*me. If I could move, I would touch him, but I **can't** move. I feel the warmth of a hand on my head. I know that energy! It's my son Michael! I hear my indrawn breath.*

"Michael," I cry silently. "You've been gone from me for over twenty years. And now you stand in front of me..." My grief and my joy are overwhelming. I am shaken to my depths, searching for words. Suddenly, there is a lifting of the pressure on my head, and I know I have received an enormous blessing. I am filled with love. And Michael is gone.

I stay quiet, wondering if I am hallucinating. I am, after all, overtired, nervous, and in the first stages of romantic love.

Lance touches me on the shoulder, and I open my eyes. He motions me toward the door. I assume our time is up and get to my feet. My knees are weak. I hope I have not cried out aloud.

In front of the church, Lance tells me he's just had a strange experience. He takes my hands in his and looks into my eyes, telling me he's felt a hand of blessing on his head. "It was your son."

So early in our meeting, we have been gifted with the approval and blessings of my child in the other realm. I cannot describe the ecstasy. There are places in time in your life that will remain touchstones forever. This is one of those. If I ever doubt that Lance and I were brought together for a purpose, including doing our work, I recall the presence of Michael and ask where these doubts are coming from. They are always in my own insecurity or the intentional interference of others.

Birth

Into this life I came, caught in a whirlwind
of pain, spiraling down into myself, into my self.
That is, until the day I lifted clear, saw sun painting
streaks across the now quiet clouds where they lay,
chastised, beneath me. Rain fell—no, not exactly;
that would be too strong a thing to name rain. That sifting
down of soft, wet ghost mist caressing my bowed head,

a blessing by echo, more significant than the flood
or manna falling on the Israelites.

My son, manna from heaven

Michael's presence in the church, his hand on my head, gave me direct experience of his energy. I recognize whenever his presence is nearby through the energy in my space. Everyone has their own vibration, their own tuning fork, their own song.

We can train ourselves to receive these energies in gratitude once we stop asking the *why* and *how* questions. Be open once you have trained yourself to discern one type of energy from another, not before. One of the main factors in disease and exhaustion of care-givers is their open channels to energy. I'll discuss this in Part Four.

Think of yourself as an incandescent power, illuminated and perhaps forever talked to by God and His messengers.

—Brenda Ueland

What Next? Jerome

For five years I have had several experiences with someone who is mentioned in the acknowledgments and introduction for this book. His name is Jerome. During the time I have felt his palpable presence, I have decided that he is a guide; a figment of my imagination; or even a deliberate attempt by dormant guilt to reach out to my Catholic background! Anything but acknowledge that he was asking much more of me. Jerome's first appearance was during a meditation class I attended at the home of a wonderful psychologist named Jill McCann. After my divorce, I had been diagnosed with a breast tumor. I also lived with a chronic condition that ranged from mildly painful to unbearable. Meditation had literally become a life-saving practice for me, and Jill's group was a healing group. As she began that night's meditation, she asked that we send love down on the earth.

I struggle with the wandering of my mind as the music filters through. Visualizing the planet is huge! The world is filled with so much tragedy, so much illness—where do I begin? I imagine rose-colored light surrounding my heart, then my body, then the room and the house. Suddenly, I'm flying into the night sky, raining that light down on our beautiful earth. I don't sense tragedy and illness, but hope. Ever since I saw my mother planet from space, she has confirmed a belief in beauty and creation. My heart swells with love for her and her inhabitants. I am truly enjoying the sensation of flying.

Gradually I return to my body, settling gently onto the couch in Jill's living room.

It is then that we began the meditation I describe in the *Introduction* to this book.

Jill asks us to enter the sacred pyramid, which is the fifth dimension or higher—she calls this the Christ consciousness, our higher self. I see the pyramid clearly above me. The capstone is filled with an undulating rainbow; a crystal projects up and down, the down pointing above a crystal table. I am lying, somehow, on the table. Surprisingly, the material that looks like crystal fits like a soft mold around my body, changing into a reclining chair. It is so comfortable! Vibrant pink and purple flow from the material through my body, and I see an angel at my head and feet, vibrating silver and purple sound-light. I am enveloped from below by a purple flame, energetic but not hot. I feel as if I'm being cleansed. I hear that my energy and higher purpose for the year is love and kindness, especially to myself, represented by purple and rose vibrations.

The air in the room is charged; the roof disappears; the heavens are chiming with blessings. I hear a voice saying: "I've been waiting for you since you were a child."

*I see him as he comes near. He is wearing a hooded robe, his gentle intelligent eyes compassionate in the shadows. He holds up a book. I can see green, maybe velvet, but it is covered with mist and I can't read the title. He brings me closer and I see the cover—*The Promise. *The book is decorated with gold markings. "Be gentle, be loving. Teach! Tell about the Truth and The Promise." And he was gone.*

I'm dumfounded by the reality I feel in this meditation. He is real. I hear his voice, I feel and sense the texture of the book, and I have a profound curiosity about the markings. But his words chill me. Tell what truth? About what promise? As he disappears, I cry out: "Who are you?"

The answer goes into my heart. "My name is Jerome."

I hear Jill's voice calling me, and I reluctantly leave the incredible energy of the pyramid. I sit in stunned silence as she asks if anyone has anything that they want to share. After two others share their experience, I open my eyes and speak. This is a safe place, and if I can't tell the truth here, where would it ever happen? The room is hushed as I tell them what happened. When I'm finished, several women say they have profound feelings of accuracy in what I describe, and they think I'd better look into the meaning of this appearance. No one has a clue as to who Jerome might be, or what the book resembles. We are filled with questions.

Since You Were a Child

"I've been waiting for you since you were a child." This speaks to a profound belief I have held my whole adult life. Children are born connected to the mystical, to the place of their origin. I felt this as a child and saw this in the eyes of my own children. "When I was a child I caught a fleeting glimpse." How I mourned its passing. I did not know how to nurture it. I had a wonderful opportunity to see this again in the eyes of my grandchildren. Look into the eyes of a newborn wiggling every moveable part of her body in the effort to communicate, and you are aware of a great wisdom. Babies still have knowledge of the *before birth* and are longing to share. How ironic that we've lost our ability to hear their wisdom.

My beautiful niece, Lisa, died before her first birthday, and she never lost the connection. She seemed to know that there was no point in joining a group that she would soon be leaving to go back home. Looking into her eyes was receiving a blessing.

Up until the age of five or so, imaginary friends are not unusual if mom and dad haven't discouraged them. Many believe these friends to be contacts for the child from a place before birth. Going back to my own earliest childhood memories doesn't evoke that connection, except for the permissible presence of my tiny guardian angel. Why do we forget? Many authors discuss this at length, including those who feel that the connection to the mystical birth remains with children until the soft fontanel of their skull closes, and then life on earth takes over. What a lovely and mysterious thought. Others believe that children of great creativity and imagination live part of their lives between the worlds, thus appearing to be distracted and requiring medication to focus them in the "real." Those who guess at the strings holding us to other worlds are only experts who guess. No one really knows, but new science points to this scenario as a real possibility.

∾ᴐᴑ

Half the misery in the world comes of want of courage to speak and hear the truth plainly.

—Harriet Beecher Stowe, novelist & abolitionist

ᴄᴐᴑ

Harriet helps when I lose my courage to speak. I am being told to tell the truth, and since what I am about to speak to is so disturbing to me, it is part of *my* truth. In light of the above paragraphs about children, I am concerned about the over-control of parents in the early stages of their child's life. When, if ever, is the child going to have time to just *be* if we begin to orchestrate their being from the time they are in the womb? I have no objection to people playing Mozart to their unborn children—the child can dream with Mozart in the background. But there are forms of control that begin at or before birth, touted by well-meaning or hungry authors who advise you on how to stimulate your child's potential. I will give one example, and I won't name the program.

I was in my doctor's office and a mother and dad came in with a four-month-old child: an adorable boy. He immediately locked eyes with Lance and his curiosity was vivid on his face. Suddenly, his mother had him upside down by two arms and was gently shaking him. He tried to get his head around under his arm to continue his perusal of the strange being sitting next to me, but was then slung around the other way, his face in his mom's belly, just missing the metal chair arm. The dad pretended to be asleep, obviously not connected to this project; I worried the mother was deranged. A patient, very pregnant, came out of the doctor's examination room and was caught by the sight of the child.

"How adorable," she said softly. "How old is he?"

The mother shared the age and immediately pointed out a web site where the pregnant mother could go to learn to get a "leg up" on her child's growth and intelligence while she was still pregnant. The exercises she was doing with her son were part of the program. She explained how babies are not supposed to see well for six weeks, but her child had perfect vision in three, thanks to her work with him.

"He's in the ninety-eighth percentile," she announced proudly.

I felt sick to my stomach, a sure signal in my body of something not quite right in my world. How do we dare to put a child in competition with other children before they're even five months old? Or before they're even born? What kind of disappointment will a parent have who gives birth to a child who does not *measure up* to their early efforts? Please hear me when I say this concern comes from my heart, as it does from the hearts of mothers who connect with these programs. It is an example of how disconnected we are from our own wisdom and how desperately we want to do our best for our children. These parents are not listening to the needs of their child or their own intuition but have become part of the culture of gurus who will tell us what we must do, and on whom we depend for the guidance on how to do it. That is why my book is only telling you how to listen to *yourself and your own intuition*, which will direct you to the right path and the right teachers for you.

Who are the people promoting this and making money at it? What about the child who is *not* in the ninety-eighth percentile? Are they going into preschool with a label on their chests? Before you think I'm against early learning for children, I'm not. But, and this is big, all human beings have their own timeline, their own path, and their own need for solitude and quiet. Soon enough, they are regaled with radio, TV, elevator music, open car windows that blast our ears with "music," and headsets of their own that blunt their eardrums and tune out their parents. Can't this early gift of time, before the world floods in, include a little space to just react, play, or watch the sun's rays coming in the window and working down the wall?

Much research shows these children have a head start and then everything catches up. I don't care about that. Good nutrition, plenty of sleep, and a peaceful environment are the main needs of a growing child.

You don't need to move their arms and legs around unless they have a condition that requires it. Babies spend most of their waking time stretching, squirming, drooling, and smiling. They can put their foot in their mouth, for heaven's sake! Enjoy it!

At one of Lance's teachings, a client talked about her recent experience with some hyper-driven teenage girls. She was telling them about her teen years, between thirteen and fifteen, and what that looked like in the early sixties. She described riding her bike through country lanes, sitting under a tree with her sketch pad, playing jacks. The girls were struck with longing. "Oh, that sounds so *good*," one of the girls sighed. "When did you have the time?"

Much has been written about the over-scheduled child, his computer, his lack of neighborhood connections, her four sport participation or goal-driven activity. I don't need to elaborate. In the name of love, we are exhausting our children and depriving them of their childhood. And it begins with *our* frantic pace as we are their role models. Brave parents who say no to some electronics, optional bedtimes during the week, and take responsibility for nutrition will not be totally popular with a hormone-driven teen. So what? That's part of the job. We are not their buddies; we are their parents. In most cases, parents are so exhausted that giving in is a choice they make to preserve their sanity. They, too, have to re-evaluate their goals and choices. Perhaps the bigger house, the bigger car, the plasma television, or the fancy vacation isn't a healthy trade-off. Taking time to find your Promise and your Truth will reveal much about the family's direction.

According to Leann Birch, PhD, professor of human development and family studies at Pennsylvania State University, whose own research has focused on five-year-old girls with eating problems: "Daughters get their attitudes toward food from the mother...negative behavior and attitudes by the mother can influence her." In other words, if mom is constantly denigrating herself and her body and going on diets, her daughter will do the same.

"Some of my patients who are just out of nursery school, tell me they're fat," says Ira Sacker, MD, co-author of *Dying to be Thin*.

And this is just about food, a subject that has created a national epidemic of anorexia and bulimia and nursery school children who weigh themselves daily, finding themselves unacceptable. What about mom and dad constantly prodding the little one to practice his brain growth? Instilling into our children the warrior attitude that they must be best, brightest, thinnest, and first—even at five months—is a message they hear whether it is verbal or not. Please, let our children be what God intended them to be—let them dream, be little mystics, and know they are loved. If you hear a lot about *mom* in this, you're right. We are still not at the stage where researchers are going to find both parents equally responsible. What fathers do with sons as they grow, particularly in relation to sports and measuring up, is another story.

Once we are beyond babyhood, we can find the stories and myths told from earliest time. Parents can read these to us until we are old enough to find them for ourselves. These stories lead us on the path, offering many clues. Because there is so much we don't know, and so much we make up to cover the gaps, we have trouble finding our truth. Some of our cover-ups are theories and some are religions, but there is more to know. When we begin to look inside, or when we are forced to look at the unusual as it occurs in our lives, some of us suspend disbelief and look for connections. Many of us, for long, short, or lifetime periods, accept what we are told and stop seeking. Yet even the most fundamental religious texts and practicing adepts encourage seeking, *inside as well as outside!*

Make your home in me, as I make mine in you,
I am the vine, you are the branches.
Whoever remains in me, with me in him,
bears plentiful fruit.
—John 17:21, 22

Earth and Heaven are in us!
—Mahatma Gandhi

Children are often the keys to our mystical doors, and sometimes they remind us of our own young experiences, happenings that we have pushed behind the veil. If we encourage daily time for quiet, not so much *noise* in the child's world, and a healthy attitude toward their experiences, children will frequently teach *us*. I have two nephews who are very in tune with more than one world. Some would say they "bleed through the boundaries." The elder, Sebastian, and I had met rarely in his young life, but I remembered him especially for one visit to my home. He asked me, very devoutly, if he could have some "beautiful cheese," referring to a block of golden cheddar residing in my fridge. Sebastian was still seeing beauty in every part of the Universe.

A couple of years went by, and I didn't see Sebastian. His family had moved out west and then back to North Carolina. One day his mom called to tell me a story.

She was saying bedtime prayers with her son, and he was doing the usual litany of "God bless Mommy and Daddy, Grandma, my brother," and the current family dogs. Then he asked if he could pray for Aunt Terry and her kids. (That would be me.) My niece was surprised, but always honoring her children's ways of being, said certainly. She knew we hadn't been together in years and wondered where this notion came from.

> *"What are her children's names, Mommy? I forgot."*
> *"Well," she replied, "there's Michelle, Paul, Catherine, Christopher, and Mary."*
> *He thought for a moment and said, "Aunt Terry has another child, Mommy."*

My son, Michael, had died many years before Sebastian's birth. His mother hadn't thought to include him. So she told him what she knew about Michael.

> *And then he said, "Michael talks to me, Mommy."*
> *Through her shock, she asked him, "About what, Sebastian?"*
> *"I can't tell. It's just for me."*

For weeks after, he prayed every night for my family and me. Then, one night, he left us out. "Don't you want to pray for Aunt Terry and her family?" Jennifer asked.

> *"Who's Aunt Terry?" replied a sleepy Sebastian.*

❦

Numberless are the world's wonders!
—Sophocles (495–405 BC)

❦

His visitations had ended, for that time. Later, my family would return to his prayers and Michael would talk to him again, but there was never a hint of the conversation. This child's younger brother illuminates the family with his memories of places he's lived (unknown to his parents) and accurate descriptions of the life there many centuries past. For some reason, certain children continue to part the veil, or have it parted for them, and the lucky ones live in families like this where their visions are honored, not ridiculed. How many others are there who have had this knowing taken from them by harsh words or even harsher actions or the beneficent application of medications? It would be wonderful if we could all meditate and recover our child's mind and recapture that openness.

The Green Book

So, with crossing the veils and the wonders of the world in mind, I return to my experience with Jerome. The night of Jill's group, as I went to bed, I asked guidance in my dreams to discover the identity of Jerome. Just before I drifted into sleep, I felt a nagging familiarity with the book. Somewhere I had seen it. Where? As I dropped off, I remembered, and re-dreamed the story.

In 1998, I had gone to a therapist/hypnotist to look for the origin of an incident that kept repeating itself in the relationship with my mate, Lance. This is the movie-like experience I had under hypnosis, which took me to an earlier life—a surprise to me, but not to her. I fully expected the situation to be connected to my childhood or earlier relationships.

I am a young girl, around twelve years of age. Based on my clothing, it is sometime in the Medieval period. I am brushing the hair of a beautiful, haughty woman in her bedroom—the room is lush and rich with fine fabrics and aglow with candles and a vigorous blaze in the fireplace. The fire doesn't warm me. I am clammy with dread. The brush slips from my wet hand and the woman slaps me and sends me away. I know I am this woman's maid, but she is also my enemy.

I move to another scene, and I am in the library of the same house where a loving father figure is teaching me. He seems secure in his position as lord of all his lands, elegant in a dark brown the color of chocolate, trimmed in gold, but he locks the library door when I arrive for my lessons; others are

39

more powerful than he. I work in his house as the serving girl of his wife. He hasn't acknowledged me, but I know from the kitchen gossip that he truly is my father. My mother, according to the cook, was a seamstress on the adjoining estate. She died giving birth to me.

His hazel eyes are sad, and he warns me again about the dangers of a girl knowing how to read. He is all that stands between me and disaster. I fear the day I lose his protection.

In the next scene, he is dying. I am fifteen. He sends for me and tells me that I am in danger and must flee. When he is gone, he says, others will tell his wife who I am and she will have me banished or killed. There is a special book locked in a cabinet behind the bookshelves that I am to take with me. He gives me a key, kisses me good-bye, and tells me he will always be there with me. I hear his wife coming down the hall and escape by a side door. A fog of grief shrouds my heart. I find the book in the library. It is green like moss in the deep part of the forest and covered with symbols. The title is The Promise.

I run to the stables, where there is a servant boy my age who has befriended me. I tell him the truth of what is happening. He throws a blanket across a horse and boosts me up. We hear the sound of mounted men coming into the courtyard, and the shrill voice of my mistress rising over the click of hooves and neighing of horses. She is telling them I have stolen something. The boy jumps on the horse behind me and we race for the nearby forest. Our lives are worth nothing if we're caught. The soldiers are behind us and closing fast as we enter the dark sweet home of the trees. I look for a place to hide the book before they catch us.

Without warning, the trees retreat and we are in a luminous world, the same place but a different time. The air is pristine and smells of pine. We see people in long robes walking to and fro, books in their hands, sharing knowledge and love without fear. I recognize the energy of the boy on the horse as my mate in this life.

I opened my eyes in the hypnotherapist's office. For a confused few minutes, I was unsure of who and where I was. I didn't understand the message, and I never went back.

This story went into a subterranean place as I lived my life, wrote my books, and went back to sleep. I took from the experience only one thing: my mate and I had common interests in books, spirituality, and the mysteries of mysticism, and had shared these in another time and place. It wasn't until years later, at the Jean Houston Mystery School, that I recognized, again, the parting of the veil.

The morning after the experience at Jill's house and recalling the story of the young girl, I went to the Internet and began the search for Jerome. Several entries came up on St. Jerome, the great teacher who had translated the Bible into Latin. For many years I have written about the women of the Bible who were unnamed or maligned by the writers/ interpreters. Pope Gregory, who assigned the word "prostitute" to Mary Magdalene long after the Bible was written, comes to mind. My first poetry chapbook had been titled *Lot's Wife*. It had always troubled me that a woman of such import, according to the story, had no name.

What could St. Jerome, the recorder of that very Bible, be asking of me? What was the Truth? What was the Promise? I had read widely on myth and spirituality, and teach workshops on recovering your passion and purpose, being in your right place, walking your walk. Was I not already telling my truth? But he had said: "Teach the Truth and the Promise." I am not a philosopher or theologian. I must have the wrong Jerome.

I put all of this aside to finish my novel, *A Time to Reap*, the book in which I subconsciously named a character Jerome. Months passed and my daily pain didn't go away. I had exhausted the route of doctors, surgeons, and medications. I was in a "dark night of the soul," a place of questioning God and the Universe. Why give me the work and no means to do it? It was getting more and more difficult to do my daily chores, let alone the *big work* I was being asked to do. I experienced that "going down into the depths" that has been taught as a spiritual path since 3500 BC, and before. From the horrific tortures of Inanna's descent and the Epic of Gilgamesh, to Jacob wrestling the angels on the ladder and modern fairy tales, we know the depths of the human psyche and human suffering. Even with those previous stories to guide me, I had not imagined how far into the darkness I had to go. It had seemed to me that the death of my child was sufficient, but I had not completed *my* part of the journey. About this time, I met a healer named Kate McKenna. I had several sessions with her and then, one day, a strange and wonderful thing happened.

Kate is trying to put a CD in her player, one that I requested, that always accompanies my treatment. The door of the CD player keeps opening and closing compulsively, refusing to accept the CD. As she fiddles with it, I hear voices in my head say: "We want Gregorian chant." Voices in the head are not unusual during healing work, but Gregorian chant is a remnant of my Catholic years that I have no desire to hear. I'm trying to relax and heal, not to mention that I'm royally ticked off at God and her representatives on earth! I say nothing.

Finally, the machine accepts the quiet calm CD and Kate begins my treatment. I look forward to the nap I fall into during this hour of healing work, but about five minutes in, Kate stops working and lays a quiet hand on me, startling me awake. She tells me something really strange is going on.

"This table," she says, "is surrounded by monks in brown robes. They are shoulder to shoulder. There's hardly room in here for me!" Kate has no fear of the other side of the veil, only curiosity. "One of them says he has a message I need to give to you. He's holding an open book, and pointing to a page. He says I need to read it to you." She clears her throat and speaks. These are the words she says:

"Walking in your truth is perfection and the way of the light.
No one who walks this path is ever alone. Truth is the spark
of all essence, and essence is the spark of all Truth.
The way to the Promise is by way of the Truth."

She looks down on my rigid form. "Do you have a clue what all of this means?"

Did I have a clue? Of course I did. All of the covering over and avoiding had come to an end. This was the third time that I had been led, through the kind hands of other women, to my work. I still didn't have a guide book, but I had a guide and I was now open to him—sort of! In the meantime, I had a retreat to teach, another three months of promotion to do for my novel, and a poetry class for third graders to develop and present with Lance. And my health was no better. I would begin when the time was right. Meanwhile, I took notes on all the things that were happening and filed them under "future book." Oh! There are none as deaf as those who *will not* hear.

In January, 2005, my dear Lance gave me a birthday gift of study with Jean Houston, a deep-rooted desire I had shared with him when we met. Following my registration, I received a letter telling me to consider well what I wanted from the school. She also suggested I ask in my dreams for my quantum guide. There was no doubt in my heart or soul; my purpose in going was to find the Truth of my work and service, and what it was Jerome was truly asking of me.

My work with women is satisfying and joyful, but felt separate from my charge by Jerome in relation to *The Book*. In the incredible mystical space created by Jean and her staff, I began to allow my judgments about borders, time, and connections to leak out of my left brain. Instead, I allowed for synchronicity and for remembering. In my meditations, I asked the question: "What have we been promised?" There are many things in scriptures of the major faiths that claim to be promises God made to "His people." We have been promised Heaven for good behavior; Hell for bad behavior; true love through fidelity and constancy; the Promised Land through Faith. But bad things happen to good people and vice versa. We all have many examples of that in our own lives.

The promise of this seems to be that we will handle both the good events and the bad events in the way we choose, and that will have its own consequences. All of this came from my logic, not my knowing. Part of the truth is that moral truths are taught to us through spiritual traditions, and these are sometimes ignored in the search for the factual truth, such as where and when our teachers were born, and who they talked, walked, and lived with. Their basic teachings are ignored by those who would use them only as tools for debate.

Certainly my memory of a time when the veil parted, and I could see the reality of another world, opened me to a larger teaching, thus a larger Promise. We are not alone, we never were, and we've been told this over and over so many times it's a wonder we haven't just been abandoned. Jean has a wonderful visual image of us in the Universe. She talks about the laboratory where those who are new and clumsy are separated from the other scientists. Where these newbies reside is called the skunk works. And here we are, we humans, at the farthest possible end of the Milky Way in the farthest possible spot in our galaxy—the skunk works. Her implication is clear, at least to me; we are young, we are learning, and we are dangerous to the rest of the Universe. We have a lot of catching up to do, and we could fail miserably if we don't change—now.

When moral and spiritual teachings are ignored in favor of interpretation and ownership, we have a society with nothing to hold to. Look around you and you will see the results of this blindness. The truth is, the teachings are simple, as I was to find out.

Following my first weekend with Jean, I opened myself nightly to dreams that would clarify my purpose and my calling. Finally, one night in March, 2005, I sounded off to my guides and whoever else was in my vicinity. I told them I'd waited and prayed for information, that I was willing, but all I got was the continued presence of the book, the instructions that I was supposed to write this book, and no guidance on what I was to write. "If you're serious," I griped, "give me a dream, or something, that will tell me what it is I am to do." The next morning, it happened.

I awoke to a voice which said: *"Good morning, Beloved. Shall we begin?"*

The voice was like a warm bath: comforting, supportive, and totally calming. I couldn't write fast enough for the words that came, and yet I could. Time *slowed* for me. The resulting dialogue, for that is how I received it, became the nucleus for this book. Originally, I received poems, then conversations, and again, poems. I have experienced Grace in a gift so generous I can't find the words to express my gratitude. I am so blessed to be the vessel for this material, and I feel a huge responsibility to present it as it was meant to be presented.

The few I have confided in, since they were to be mentioned in the book, asked if it was channeled. To me, that means we all have conduits, channels, pipes, openings—whatever you want to call them—to the mystical, to our original joining with our spirits. These connections are truly clogged with the sludge of daily life. When we open these connections through intentional prayer, meditation, visualization, or any other means, we are in touch. Whether we are in touch with our higher selves, God, spiritual guides, or angels is open to individual interpretation or opinion.

Mystical and religious writings refer to the Beloved as an aspect of the self still in contact with divine and eternal love. Since I have been aware of that connection as it is maintained by young children, it was easy to understand. As I said, I have only to look into the eyes of babies and young children to see the luminous presence of the spirit. Now I know we can regain the connection, since that is necessary to reveal our Promise. What a long road and burden of work had led me here. I would like to know if it has to be so difficult. My answer is that it is different for everyone. For me, it is enough that the "Roto-Rooter of soul work" finally cleared out some sludge and possibilities bloomed into Grace. Also, I remind myself of the joy I have experienced in the journey. It was never just a burden of work. On good days, I knew that.

There are days when I have no pain and everything flows like spring water. Then there are days when I doubt and think the voice will leave me, and it does. But I know this work is being given to me for a reason. As long as I am faithful to the purpose, all closings are temporary and created by fear. May I be of service to the beauty of this blessing and may you receive it with love. You will possibly feel something akin to what I wrote about in this poem as I experienced my awakening.

Initiation

Fire!
She's on fire! Flames lick
her thighs, flare toward the curtains.
Heat!
Hot, red, searing reflected
in white silk, auroras of blue Sulfur.
Wings!
Can it be wings flaring
like dragon's breath beneath her sweaty
back? She is about to
Fly!
Wind lifts her above the bed,
updraft so hot she sizzles
then drifts through the window,
wings and curtains flaring behind her

Like Persephone's bridal veil.
Cooled
by evening, she sails on the breeze till
near dawn, then returns to her bed
trailing gray clouds and rain drops
to dampen the sheets, cool the mattress.
Morning
no trace remains of embers or smoke;
only an open window, singed
linens, and the softly breathing woman,
mist rising from her skin, pomegranate
seeds dappling her hair.

Part Two:

THE DIALOGUES

∽⚭∼

And did you get what you wanted from this life, even so?
I did.
And what did you want?
To call myself beloved, to feel myself
beloved on the earth.

—Raymond Carver (as he was dying), "Late Fragment"

∽⚭∼

Good Morning, Beloved. Shall We Begin?

What Matters: A Dialogue

And I ask you,
What matters?
Love matters.
What else can be said?
Well, it is in how we love.
And that is?
Without judgment;
in total acceptance.
Am I a saint, then?
It is in the attempt, Beloved.
Look into the true eyes
of your friend. No, not the
latched gate that faces town,
but the inner rooms
where fear lies down;
the bed of loneliness only
he knows, the scraps
on the table of desire.
See with the eyes of love,
Beloved, and the gifts

49

are as the seeds of the Papaya;
many, polished, teak beauties
strung on the necklace
of eternal joy.

Dialogue II

And what about fear? Sometimes, I am so afraid.
Beloved, there is so much to say.
The birds in the chimney are safe
from the cat; but what of the fire
in the grate? Act without fear,
for no place is safe or dangerous.
It is just place.
How shall I know where to go?
Go where your soul leads you.
That is the only place. Don't
ask questions or seek comfort.
Just go! You will be guided;
you will have what you need.
All else is chaff on the ground.
When you return, your face
will shine with the oil of knowledge
and radiate the glow of your spirit.

Dialogue III

Tell me who you are!
So, Beloved. You ask for a name.
I am all that is. So, I am you
and you are me and we are all
there is. But we are *they* also,
so how can you not love all who
are? How does one name this?
Now you are asking the questions!

True! You have called this one God,
The Universe, the Secret One. I
laugh at that! I am no secret. Look
at the flowers, the trees, the birds,
a cow for Heaven's sake! Where
is the secret? The love that falls
on you when you grieve in the early
hours of morning is no secret. I am
always here. I am. That is all
you need to know. It is enough.
You say I must love all who are, as you are there in them and so am I. It
is always the same question. What about Evil?
Evil is part of all there is, as is laughter,
stupidity, gentleness, and prejudice. Some
have chosen to carry more of one of these
qualities than others. Only great Good
can overcome Evil. The Universe is moving
toward Good, always. When you look in
the eyes of prejudice and see beyond it to
Good, you are acknowledging All There Is,
not just one facet of the jewel.

Dialogue IV

Good morning, Beloved. What old habit would you like to release today?
Are you going to ask the questions? I like it better when you give
the answers!
I think, for now, this works well. Begin.
I would release resentment. It fills spaces in me that could be used
for good things.
Such as?
Patience, I think.
Are they equal, resentment and patience?
Oh no. The places of storage need to be rearranged. Resentment
is stored with anger, in sharp ice crystal shards inserted in lower back

and shoulders. Those need to be emptied and dissolved. Patience is stored in the eyes and heart, also in the mouth.

I like that. What would Patience sound like?

Gentle tones; bell-like notes. The face would soften with love, because the two go hand in hand: Patience and Love in one house.

What is Patience, Beloved? Is it forbearance?

No. Forbearance says, "I put up with your thoughts or actions." Patience says: "I hold a space with your thought or action and look for the truth of it."

And where is the Ego during all of this?

Tied up in a corner! Sorry. The ego is relaxed, aware, and discerning. Patience is finite. I don't believe in killing the ego. God gave it to us for a reason.

Ah, good! So your other senses, like discernment, will say when patience has run out?

Not run out, but been excused for the time being. It might be time to meditate or, at least, be alone. Patience sometimes runs up against right action.

Explain?

I might be patient in a situation where someone needs to tell their story. If they have told the same story over and over with no desire, yet, to heal or change the story, I must withdraw. This is not Patience but Respect; Respect for their place in time and mine.

Ah, Respect—another powerful piece of the human puzzle. You have this, I think. You are ready to go into imagistic meditation, are you not? Remember to remove those shards of resentment and anger with patience and respect for what your body thought it was doing for you as you release and heal. We have accomplished much.

Dialogue V

I desire the blossoming of my Soul. Can you help me?

Beloved, you hear my voice. There is no water to sprinkle on the flower of your Soul—it is all about *light*; the light of forgiveness; the light of love; the sunshine of non-judgment. You open petal by petal as you give of yourself in service to love and spirit. Desire opens you, love releases the velvet scent recognized by other Souls. It is a garden like no other. Taste the colors! Smell generosity! In this way, Heaven is revealing herself to you.

What action can I take right away? I do want to be pleasing to spirit.

Every action you take leads you toward or away from your Soul's growth. There is no mistaking which is which. You body is the sensing device for your spirit. It tells you when your action is good or bad for you through its finely tuned feedback system—a generous gift from God. Increase your awareness of its signals as they are instant and recognizable. When you act against your spirit, you will experience distress somewhere in your body. It is different for each of you. Joy, contentment, relief are the signals of right action in your sensory self. Awareness is all that matters.

Dialogue VI

"I stand ready to open to grace."

This tightness hurts. *From neck to anus, clenched in fear. What will happen if I let go? What is it I need to release?*

My child, it is for your body to say. Ask! Neck, what is it you hold? What or who is it that you fear to bend before?

Authority. I don't want to be told what to do or think or say.

Good! Now, ask again! Back, what is stored in the stiffness? Where is the subtle stretch you found in yoga when you were fifty years old?

Pain—or fear of pain. Especially in my low back, coccyx, anal muscles, butt muscles.

You make progress. Now ask your legs, your feet, aching and sore. What is there?

Standing hurts, walking hurts. Forget running, leaping, and dancing! I am held in a vise.

What is it? Where is the music?

Sadness? Rage? Where did it come from? What is it? Who is it?

You have done enough for now. Daily, go through your body. Get to know it. It will talk to you.

I will meditate on this. I stand ready to open to Grace.

The greatest sin of all is the unlived life.

—John O'Donohue

Dialogue VII

What is the unlived life?

It is the failure to enjoy every facet of your gifts, to settle for routine and safety and to deny your character.

What's wrong with people just relaxing?

Oh, Beloved, you try to trick yourself with words. Closing your eyes and ears to the music of the Universe is an active denial of your Soul's purpose. Do you think the maker of all this beauty and passion meant for you to deny it? When a child stands in front of a machine with a fake gun, blowing people up to while away the time, did he not have other choices like read a book, ride a bike in the fresh air, learn to play an instrument, write a poem, draw or paint a picture, throw or catch a ball? Surely it cannot be the video game—or, for his parent, the television. We are called. We have free will to answer or not.

Does that mean I shouldn't go to the movies?

You know that there are movies that will raise your knowing of places and people or your understanding of myth and story, or make you laugh. Others will only stoke the furnace of the Shadow. You do not need me to tell you this.

You sound annoyed. I'm sorry. I just seem to be having a hard time focusing right now. I feel like I am a thorn in the side of many who are just content to be. I'm always pushing for "doing."

Some *being* is necessary—you know this also. But being has purpose: to be in silence, so you can hear spirit, is being with purpose, as you are right now; resting simply to rest has purpose. Acting without the knowing that comes from being is hollow. You understand this, but when you are stressed, as you are now, it all sounds difficult. Truly, it is simple. Just remember to breathe and listen. All will return to you.

this "breathe and listen?" I am told to listen
my soul. I lie on my bed and close my eyes,
nping life to all parts of me, being steady and
ese years. I say, heart, speak to me. Heart, tell
me your story.

Heart, Tell Me Your Story

I've been waiting a long time for you to ask.
I have loved well and much, sometimes
unwisely, but always with a warmth like
a hearth on a winter's night. I have been
broken, twice in a way that even God
wouldn't heal for a long time...years,
in fact. Small fractures healed, scarred,
and went unnoticed, those two were
jagged cuts with a dull knife—uncivilized
and cruel. Look closely and you'll see wide
white scar tissue in the shape of lightning
bolts. The doctors say I have to work harder
to pump the blood. I think it is to remind me
of joy by reminding me of pain. Without
both, how can we know which to choose?
Someday I will heal completely and the dams
of my veins and arteries will open fully. Love
will rush once again like mighty rivers.
I sing, too. It is not all tragedy. Love raised me
up the mountain more than once. I have flown,
seen fields of sunflowers undulate below me
mile after golden mile. Children have warmed
me, soft quilts of feathers folded and tucked
around me to keep winter out. Children! Their
hearts are grown from pieces of me, regenerating

beat and cell for the next family of hearts. I
am like an old barn, moonlight slanting through
the broken places in the roof that still shelters
all who need me. I am ready to give up the pain,
to open wide to love again. I need a gentle partner
to catch my fears and whisk them away. I need
a trustworthy friend, kind-eyed and warm-handed
to massage my scars with oil of almond. We hearts
are fragile but strong, like the legs of antelope.
Once broken, we must be hidden until we are strong
enough to run again, out-pace the jackal and hyena.
I think I am nearly ready. Since you ask, you must
be leaning that way too. Are you ready to take me out
again, expose me to love and danger?

Body, tell me *your* story.

On damp days, my legs ache, my feet swell,
and the sinus cavity in my right temple hurts
like a sore tooth. But I can still touch my toes and turn
my head in a way that pleases the chiropractor, even
when he shows me the spurs on my beautiful spine!
The hoof-shaped scar on my back tells
the tale of a lucky escape from cancer,
and the invisible scar on my right breast does the same.
Barbed wire sketched on my wrist tells a scarier story.
Strength lies here in hips and shoulders that carried children
and home. Pleasures of love are still alive in hidden
gardens and soft breasts shaped like tears.
Arms hold grandchildren though this round belly
will nurture no more babes. Temperature fluctuations
are frequent and surprising in this body that changes

without warning. It is always a new story, a new show.
I have traded youth for maturity and so am somewhat slow,
but I see so much more than I did when I was speeding
down life's sidewalk. I like naps now, especially when my
beloved and I nap together. We take time to rest in each other's
arms, speak slowly and tenderly of love, plans, and desires.
I am a lucky body for I have seen much, and there is so much
more I will see. Thank you.

*To me the concept of the "Beloved" conveys
not just a nice, cozy, warm relationship with
God, but one that is joyous, uplifting and
exhilarating because it is a recognition of
who I am.*

—Nina Yfiry

What an amazing thing, to speak gently and lovingly to one's own physical self. When I heard the words *the body is the tuning fork for the Universe*, it gave me a lot to think about. This body that we strive to shape, discipline, push to its limits, is constantly scanning the energy fields for information that creates our unfolding. Our ears hear spoken information, our body reacts. Our inner ear hears the music of the Universe, captured by our body. Energy flows into all receptors and is acted upon by our body. This is truly an awesome gift, God's promise that we will be all we can be if we only become aware. Close your eyes and be perfectly still. Become aware of all the energies fighting for your attention, from the breeze on your skin to the voices in your mind. The body, mind, and soul are a universe unto themselves, reaching out to the natural world, the cosmic world, the spiritual world, the mystical world, and the world of our creating—all at the same time. We are a huge receptor, arms open wide, unless we shut down. And then, all bets are off until we are shaken open again by a traumatic event or our own life's purpose unfolding, usually in mysterious ways.

If you feel you've shut down in some area of life, begin to awaken again by touching that other body, Mother Earth. Those of you who have been ill or suffered unbearable loss know that the energy in nature is the true healer. This doesn't come up in political discussions of saving the environment, but it is absolutely the most essential reason for doing so. Mother Earth is our healing, nurturing relative. How do we understand beauty? Who told us that when we look up at the stars, we draw in our breath and experience beauty and majesty? And who told us that trees are healing? And who told us that looking at a garbage dump, a strip-mined mountain, or wires sagging over the highway is not beautiful? There is some discernment built in, is there not? When you can, please write about the feelings you have when you are in nature, or, conversely, when you cannot be in nature.

As the dialogues continue to come—usually just upon awakening, but sometimes during the night—I realize that there are many voices. It is not Jerome, as I first thought, who talks to me. He seems to be the one who brought me the book, the title, and my reason for writing it and then left me to others. Sometimes, I have a thought in my head, as in John O'Donohue's statement about the unlived life. I love it when I hear a dialogue forming around another person's thought. Some of the speakers have identified themselves to me, others I recognize intuitively, possibly because I knew their earth energy. Science and philosophy both teach that there is no destroying energy. Therefore, the energy of those who have been here in life is still available after death. I don't know the "how" of it, but I know it's true. When I awake from a dream of my friends Pat or Jai or my mother or Michael, their energy is still vibrating in the room. There is no doubt.

Dialogue VIII

You have many questions today. You grieve. Why?

I ask myself this question. My love has had surgery—the cancer is small, curable. I'm grateful and he's grateful that we were alerted and he will be well. And yet, in the midst of this gratitude, I'm tired and I am filled with sadness.

The tired you understand—it is logical given the anxiety and work involved in this time. Ignore it. Sleep. You will both recover. The grief is something you must address. Hospitals evoke other hospitals, other crises: your son's death; your friends, Pat, Ann, and Jai. Even your mother's death, though she was not in the hospital. It is about the shortness of life, in your way of looking at time. Every illness or accident is a reminder of the fragility of humans. Each person is precious. Each person is on a path of spiritual becoming even as the body ages and becomes less in its physical perfection. When the balance tips to appreciation of the spiritual self over fear of human loss, the grief will grow less. As long as you love there will be grief, but it will be less. Holding on to life, to youth, to a place in time will only increase sadness and grief. Gracefully releasing and accepting the truth of living will lessen these emotions and increase appreciation and joy in the moment.

How do I do this?

Just as you are. Face it, ask it why, and take the next step. Give power to your spiritual body and it will soothe your emotional body. Then your physical self will do its work. Do not think that love will lessen grief. However, lack of love is a tragedy. Grief is human and empowering.

I am agitated, anxious for my *new* life to begin. What's next? Where is it?

How will I know?

Beloved, be still, for it is in stillness that you grow. Go to your quiet place. Imagine the seed in the ground, in darkness, vibrating with life energy, waiting, absorbing. Only then can the green shoot raise itself through darkness to the sun, becoming lily, onion, daffodil, or asparagus. Even so, some part stays below, still in darkness, still orchestrating the being that is becoming; and sometimes, the beauty above is nothing to the substance below—the vibrant, succulent golden carrot hiding in the dark. The way to the Promise is by way of The Truth. The way to the Light is through the fertile Darkness—not to be confused with the darkness of wrongdoing. And the truth is, everything is in everything. Naming it only makes it smaller.

After and Before

A log in the grate, call it log,
forget that it was an Oak,
knew who it was, put down
snake roots to sip the waters
of Boone creek. Oh, and Fall!
Leaves of gold, burnished
copper, reflecting October's
light like Pharaoh's tunic.
But that was then and this
is now…fire! Not tree, not
log, but fire; blazing tongues
of butterscotch, flickering
blue incense, gray smoke
to signal the Tribe that
transformation is here
and now, rising toward heaven
from a change in naming.

Dialogue IX

*I really struggle with "love your neighbor." I have seen beautiful people
who hold no anger toward anyone, separate themselves from judgments. But
they are rare! Everyone quotes Mother Teresa or the Dali Lama.*

You are drawing lines again—us and them. There are degrees of
everything.

The Truth is, it is in the trying that we grow and in the growing
that we recognize our potential. It is all about love, and there are many
different degrees of love on this planet. You know all about this, do you
not? Mother and Father love, brotherly love, friendship, love of nature,
spiritual love, love of the creator. You still have a bit to learn about love of
self, but that will come in due time. All are different in scope and feeling.
But I understand your question. It is about love of your fellow man that

you are concerned. I can only tell you that all are deserving of love, no matter how they have bent. But that love must be discerning. You must love "mankind" as directed, but unless you are a saint, you will grow into this over long periods of time. Your love for your family is an example of how it can be. Don't push yourself. You will find the way through in your own good time. Write about it, Beloved. You learn best that way.

Mankind

Taken as a whole, can I truly love
All? Or is that a false, idealistic,
and easy loving? One at a time,
there's the rub! She who talks
too much, overcomes all other
voices; result? Irritation. See
the goddess in her, the child
who was never heard, a performer
with no training—a job at Wal Mart.
The man next door who watches,
peers through windows as if they
were crystal balls; incensed at his
invasions? Just possibly, through
God's eyes, a lonely soul finding
meaning in those bonded by family.
Sometimes, just a loud mouth and
a nosy neighbor with no story
to tell, but I doubt that explanation.
The government of men who see
through the narrow end of the prism;
black/white, us/them. My Sadness
at lost possibilities is a form of love.
It gives credit for the presence
of God, ignored or perverted, but

present. It recognizes the diamond
focus as mistaken but believed.
This is a hard-won kind of love
that must be coaxed back over
and over again. The multinational,
the business owner who cheats
the poor and treats the earth as his
personal marble? Anger. This one
is more difficult. Love for those
fair of heart and accounting reaps
more love because they are not other.
For now, that will have to do.
I learn to love through veneer, beyond
mirror, beneath layers of neglect. Like
an antique chair lovingly restored,
polished to a high gloss; a treasured
piece passed down from the family
into my love, finally, to God's hands.

I am struggling mightily with this concept of loving all as part of the one. My intellect and my spiritual guidance acknowledge that this is true. My ego, the font of discernment, puts my practice of this knowledge on a leash. To support non-judgment, I remember the wonderful poem "The Ways We Touch" by Miller Williams. One of my favorite lines, a Truth beyond argument, reads:

> "You do not know what wars are going on
> down there where the spirit meets the bone."

Dialogue X

You call on me so soon. What is happening?
I think I know how to love, and then I realize a lot of it is surface.

I can lavish love, feel called to love, reject love, and then I'm totally confused about love.

Love is a word, not an action.
Being loving is action.
Whatever your situation, slow down.
Think about the most loving thing to do under the circumstances.
It could be that the most loving thing for YOU would be to leave the situation.
Are you in a social situation where words are being spoken that are repugnant to you, or a relationship that does not honor your soul?
You must learn discernment—the relative of judgment, but a necessary survival quality.
Also, you must know when you are choosing to love only that which is easy to love without judgment, such as trees and flowers!
Practice noticing on a daily basis whether you only love when it is easy and withdraw that love when it is difficult. This is a major lesson and requires you to tell the truth!

After the last two directions about love, I was in a place of deep searching and uncovered parts of myself that were not pleasant to view. I also know now that being in a place of love means giving myself some credit for the work I'm doing and not playing the "blame game." I began to notice when I was judging, when I was being discerning, and when I was confused! It is still a daily struggle to live the loving life in a wholehearted fashion, but I am at least able to *notice*, the first step to change. I read about a woman who wrote incredibly beautiful, loving books about the natural world and was about to be divorced from her husband of many years. I fantasized about her applying her nature love to her husband, and wrote the following poem.

Myopia

She loves swans and turtles
without judgment, praises
feather and shell with equal

63

luminosity. He waits, trims
his beard, whitens his smile,
reads all the books she leaves
on his bedside table.
Still, she goes on her morning
walks, deserts their warm bed,
throws him an absentminded
kiss. He knows she carries
pen and notebook, will take
careful notice of the beauty
arranged casually by Nature.
Perhaps, one day, he'll lie
down among mushrooms at
the base of the spring. Unaware,
she could begin noticing his
finer points before recognition
turned her away. Or, perhaps, she
would lie down among mushrooms.

Does anyone else relate to this? I love what comes up to teach me about my own truth when I least expect it. Sometimes I argue, saying, "That's not me. I try really hard." Yes, I try really hard, and yes, that *is* me.

Dialogue XI

Beloved, there is the Great Truth and then there is your truth—the truth for each individual life. You teach that each person must serve their purpose with passion in order to have a life of fulfillment, thus, happiness. Begin there. The larger purpose you seek will come from pursuing your knowing on a daily basis.

How do I do that through the details of a busy life?

You do this through intention and attention, as all great teachers have revealed. Through noticing signs, incidents, and words that vibrate in your body—you will know where the path truly lies. Doing what you consider mundane chores is an opportunity to open your heart and mind to messages from us. Creating simple ritual is where we live. We are always nudging and suggesting once you tell us we are welcome.

You say "we."

There are many ways of guidance provided on your journey. You are experiencing only one of them at this moment. Others are what you call déjà vu, bright ideas, epiphanies. When your skin shivers or arises in bumps or your hair lifts; when dreams stay with you as if they are realities in daily life; these are all signals a presence is guiding you. Most of these are covered by everyday business. Awareness must be practiced. Open all your receptors and practice discernment. You *must* trust your intuition, for that is what these guiding feelings are. You will know what is true and what is wishful thinking and what comes from the house of fiction once your heart is in the right place. Write it, dream it, practice it, and the truth will only become stronger.

Right now, I have words that lift my skin, that say they come from elsewhere.

Write them as you hear them, Beloved. You are hearing us.

I will write the words as I hear them. The title is Spirals.

Spirals

Belief in the power of the one
To create a difference;
the power of the word.
Belief in the power of the word
to make ritual;
the power of transformation.
Belief in the power of transformation
to inspire healing;
the power of the human spirit.
Belief in the power of the human spirit
to produce good;

the power of God.

Belief in the power of God

to create all that is;

the power of the Soul.

Belief in the power of One.

Belief in the power of One!

Dialogue XII

When you last spoke to me, you spoke about the power of one as the word, ritual, transformation, the human spirit, God, and the Soul. And yet you have told me all is one, therefore indivisible. This confuses me.

It should not, Beloved, for you have been told from the beginning that one is all and the all is one. **I am the vine of truth, growing on the gates of heaven**.

What would you have me do, or say? I find myself far away—far from the open gates.

Beloved, you wander. The path is clear but you are distracted by gaudy signs that lead you elsewhere.

How do I ignore the false signs and keep my eyes on the true path?

Stop listening to the carnival barkers shouting their slogans. None of it matters. Only the work matters, and the path is visible when you are doing the work.

What about family and friends? Are they to be seen as carnival barkers?

You mistake the path and the work as separate from the world. It is not. You know better. You teach this. Love and right action toward others is what makes the work of value and keeps you warm in your humanity. Separating the path from work and work from love is what makes humans so lonely. Do you not see? It is all one thing: me speaking; you writing; lovers loving; parents caring; friends; service to others. It is all one.

Thank you for clarity. I may veer here and there, but I know where the center is.

Do not forget to look to your poets—they are often touched by the creative hand of God.

(Here are some examples I found when I went looking!)

The kingdom of God does not come if you watch for it. Nor will anyone be able to say "it is here" or "it is there." For the kingdom of God is within you.
—Jesus of Nazareth

To see a World in a Grain of Sand
And a Heaven in a Wild Flower,
Hold Infinity in the palm of your hand
And Eternity in an hour.
—William Blake

Out beyond ideas of wrongdoing and rightdoing,
There is a field. I'll meet you there.
—Rumi

Why do you weep? The source is within you.
—Rumi

Every blade of grass has its Angel
That bends over it and whispers, "Grow, grow."
—The Talmud

It is only with the heart that one can see rightly;
what is essential is invisible to the eye.
—Antoine de Saint-Exupéry

We are the flow, we are the ebb.
We are the weavers; we are the web.
—Shekinah Mountainwater

If you look for the truth outside yourself,
It gets further and further away.
—Tung Sham

*And you who seek to know ME, know that your seeking
and yearning will avail you not, unless you know The Mystery:
for if that which you seek, you find not within yourself, you
will never find it without.*
—Doreen Valiente, "Charge of the Goddess"

So, Beloved. I have met you in the field, and I have directed you within. There is so much more than you can imagine. Your spirit will help you to play the song you were born to play, be the heart you were born to be, and love as you were meant to love.

*At first people refuse to believe that a strange new thing
Can be done, then they begin to hope it can't be done,
Then they see it can be done—then it is done and all the world
Wonders why it was not done centuries before.*
—Frances Hodgson Burnett, *The Secret Garden*

I would add that most amazing things *have* been done. We've just forgotten how to do them. In between the revelations I have been receiving, a lot of work has been going on. I study my inner self like the markings on a map, following my journey forward and backward, zigzags of my life in broad black lines and squiggly thin red ones.

I think about when I was off the track and what I did, if anything, to get back on. I hear the voice, or voices, telling me over and over: *the way to the Promise is by way of the Truth.* At every point in my life where I have denied myself by pushing the knowingness of myself below the requirements of others or the world I live in, I have experienced illness. Surviving the death of my child, my marriage, my mother, my business, and many friends required a conscious reawakening of the heart. Going back to business as usual and packaging grief in small compartments means that the part of the body where these packages are stored will break down. Notice where your aches and pains—or true illness—reside, and you will know where you store the energy of these packages of grief, anger, resentment, and loss.

Our purpose is to uncover the Truth. And when we do, we will be one with all that is, in perpetual right-doing and joy. *That is part of the Promise.* One more piece of the puzzle.

As long as we seek outside for Truth, we will live in constant wanting. That is a choice. Accumulating stuff is a sad substitute for the knowledge and peace of true knowing. Changing our looks through plastic surgery, liposuction, and other means that are not health oriented, is an attempt to create happiness through change. A man who leaves his wife for a younger woman, because his inner knowing tells him something is wrong with his life, is trying to create happiness through change. Moving from town to town in search of the right path is another example. These *do not* work. Moving for one's work or love is a different story, but unguided movement is useless. *We go where we go.*

Our energy is telling us, in the above examples, that something is wrong. Messages in the body or the heart are tips from the universe that we would do well to listen to. Keeping on in our old ways, as in doing more of the same thinking that will change our lives, is to be blind to our capabilities and possibilities. Short-term surface changes have nothing to do with our longing to be part of the greater work of our souls. They cannot replace our search for the knowledge and peace of true knowing. Such attempts will only lead to emptiness. This misdirected energy takes on many guises. Religious people who see "us versus them," in direct contradiction of their religious teaching, will continue to go deeper and deeper into loss and anger.

To fill yourself with love, compassion, service, you must first cultivate the ability to sit quietly and experience the energy of the body interacting with the universe; inner action before outer action. This alone will lead you deeper and deeper into your truth, yourself, and God. Your whole body will vibrate with joy. There may be illness or pain in your body, but you will rise above it, and if you desire, eliminate it. Most of the medieval mystics acknowledged that their bodies failed them, but they were pushing beyond what we can even imagine, spending most of their time in a place that is not of the physical. We will be what we will be— that is our path. If they had chosen to be mystics with healthy bodies, they could have done so. Their souls decided that they had lessons to learn that required emptying their physical vessel. We all have choice.

The Path to the Truth

Hold tight to the sun
Shining on a path of simple
white stones. Inhale lemon
born of patient leaves, creamy
blossoms, fruit…sacred yellow!
Come, borne on these laden
breezes of Mediterranean citrus.
Come forth, exhale into the eyes
of children; of grief; old souls
longing for home. Show them
The road to the Temple of Self,
the Church of Purpose. Your
mouth is rouged with the glow
of pomegranates; the rubies
of Paradise. It is so simple!
Breathe in, breathe out.
Your hair will vibrate with love.

Dialogue XIII

*I find myself stepping on the heels of Truth, but it is always one stride
ahead of me.*
Slow down! I can't be found at this frantic pace.
Settle, like mud to the bottom of the well. There,
deep within the echoing chamber of yourself, I can
be found in silence. I promise you will find me
when you sink into me and know I am you.
When two people meld in the act of love, there is that
momentary joining with all there is! That is the "little death,"
a small sample of the true melding—the knowing that we are all
one, all connected, all energy, all God. This is why you have been
given the gift of sexual love—not just sex for the experience, sex

for the knowing. Without love, the knowing is not there.
Sexual love is the key to experiencing the ecstasy of oneness
on a scale of one person to one person.
Imagine, Beloved, what this ecstasy could be in the Universal
oneness. Millions of one to oneness. It is not describable
in your words, but imagine the feeling. This is pure bliss,
what you are created for—the Promise of Oneness.

*My heart has spread its sails to the idle winds
for the shadowy island of anywhere.*

—Rabindranath Tagore

June, 2005. The month of June is a difficult time in the life of my
family. It is a demarcation of "with Michael and without Michael;" again,
an epic time frame as real as BC and AD. When a son or daughter dies
before the parents, it is not only the death of the body, but a vacuum
to be filled with guesses, conjecture, and myth. Who would he have
become? What would she have given the world with her talent, her
love, or her smile? What part of me would he have carried forward?
Michael's gift was to set us on the path of questioning ourselves and our
beliefs about life, death, myth, and spirituality. His appearance to Lance
and me in the church had affirmed his purpose and presence. Still, June
brought the usual psychic pain lodged in my heart. I called on my guides
to return to me, soothe my pain, and explain things!

Dialogue XIV

I am struggling. I ask for clear guidance and there is silence.

Maybe you struggle, Beloved, because we have answered you and
you have not listened.

But I am listening. Every day in prayer and meditation I call on you.

We did not say we are found only in prayer and meditation. Every
day, in small ways of being and doing, we are instructing you. When

you placed the dried lavender in the cabinet to scent the sheets, we were reminding you of ways of pleasure.

Those are everyday things—putting flowers in vases, scenting the curtains with anise and lavender to catch the breeze.

These *are* the everyday. But does everyone do this? Being tuned in to the loving things of the human life is one of the most important of spiritual practices. These are all a part of loving the world one gesture at a time. Do not mistake them as too small. A moment to stroke the arm of your loved one as you pass, intent on an errand. Loving, one gesture at a time; this is the Great Work for all souls on your planet, and especially important now. So do not reprimand yourself. Love is not often in the big things, but in the daily blessings you scatter about you like rose petals.

I am asking for clear knowledge about life and death; the purpose of my son's life and death.

These are big questions, best resolved in the small things. We are not separate—there is a bridge between all. Close your eyes and visualize only fog. This is how you see the world outside of your world. Now, see the fog lifting. There, see it? There is a bridge between you and all that is. See how sturdy it is? It has handrails. You are not separate from any part of the Universe, including your son. Sometimes it is easier to reach those in other dimensions than to reach those who sit across from you at dinner! You have been given glimpses of this. Now, it is time to see the whole picture.

You feel different. It's as if your energy has a body. And yet, you say "we."

That's because I represent the feminine in *all* her aspects. You make a mistake to assume there is only one of us. Your work requires the wisdom of many.

I've often envisioned a council in my meditations. I welcome their wisdom.

We share our knowing with you, and also our protection. You have been on the periphery of your work for many years. The time has come. Listen well. You have asked how you may serve, and we have come to tell you. You must remember what Jill told you about the responsibility you carry. You must study this and then we will work together.

Can you explain The Promise and The Truth?

In due time, my daughter. You are uncovering the Truth. The Promise will reveal itself. Follow the threads, the clues you are being given. Then ask for me again and I will come.

Who will I ask for?

I am the Sacred Female, the one who cries out for healing, for recognition of the dishonored. You have had me with you for a long time. Now is your time to serve your planet through revealing the wound and healing it. Polish the bowl, burnish the cauldron, and replace the sacred fire pit. You will have much help in this. Gaia is crying out, "I thirst!" There is a large Truth to be revealed: **the wound of the Fisher King is denial of the Feminine.**

Fulfilling Our Promise

*That which we call God may have much greater plans
for us than we could ever imagine. Of course we have
the freedom to accept or reject these plans. We can
choose to co-create with the Creator or we can deny
our inheritance and let our lives bumble along until
we are finished.*

—Dr. Jean Houston, *A Passion for the Possible*

Co-create with the Creator. This is what we do when we go to our
highest self, our highest guidance, and accept or reject our life's Promise.
We cannot fulfill the Promise without telling the Truth. I have been
brought back to my essence, the place of my suffering, and my purpose.
No matter where I turned my path, it was always waiting for me. I
saddened or angered easily over almost everything having to do with
women—such as job pay disparity, the witch trials, the suffragettes, ma-
ternity leave, marital infidelity. You name it, I was upset about it.

I went to Jill as a therapist to get this out of my mind and body. She
told me that it was not in my mind but in my heart and purpose. She explained that some people carry the burden of grief for many others, and
mine was such a case. I was shouldering a cosmic load of inequality and

unfairness for women who could not speak for themselves. It was why I felt driven to write about the women of the Bible, such as Lot's wife. She said it was part of my work to teach about these things and expiate some of the damage done to women through the ages. It was part of the problem in my marriage and earlier relationships that I couldn't "get over it."

"Teach," said Jerome. "Tell the Truth." And now, here was this powerful feminine presence telling me "the wound of the Fisher King is denial of the Feminine. Remember what Jill told you about your responsibility." So I find another part of telling my truth, a part that will engender resistance and teach me to be myself without worrying about the judgment of others. This search for truth is like a ball of string that belongs in the Guinness Book of Records. What is it I fear in the process? Why does pain and illness reappear as I hear what my path is? I am finding out that those who are guiding me are many and powerful, yet I burrow under the safety of the everyday and leave out so many truths of my path.

I have noticed that I felt the truth of my burden, the history of women, to be a challenge to the book. In other words, what I have written is for women *and* men, but my path, my promise, my truth lies through the story of women. Would this mean that fewer people would be drawn to read it, thus my purpose of reaching all who would recover their Truth and Promise would be diluted?

Through these mental gymnastics blooms my paralysis in the writing. It is not that I don't know my Truth now, and that I don't want to honor my Promise, but I'm trying to second-guess who will or won't read it. There is no way to be True to one's self with one eye on the marketplace. It is all of the spirit. I am in the process of struggling with this Truth, the familiar pain a constant companion. I lie down for a nap. Struggle within the body creates unbelievable fatigue. A familiar closure of my left ear signals the arrival of a messenger.

Dialogue XV

I can't sleep. The harder I try, the less successful I am. Now you ask me to hear you. Here I am. What is it that I need to know?

You are conflicted and unhappy. After a weekend of emotional work, you are still not telling the Truth. Even in therapeutic situations, you protect and defend yourself and all others that you love. This isn't necessary. Where the truth lies (I know—I heard it too) is within the body, lodged energetically in the cells of memory and feeling. When you deny what you need, say it is okay, you fill the cells with conflict. From this comes illness. We couldn't let you sleep until you saw this for yourself. I was chosen to direct you.

Who are you? I'm so tired. I've tried to be honest, but also tried to make things work so everyone gets what they need. What's wrong with that?

I'm the voice of your knowing, brought to you by your higher self but coming from a time you can't remember. Once you knew your purposes on the planet. You have forgotten. A gentle reminder is all that is needed. You have several purposes in life, Beloved. First is to be Love. You think that is shown in making sure everyone gets what they need, but that is secondary love. Primary love is making sure that you follow your purpose and let others see what that means. Second is to always follow your heart. When you do, you will be in right-doing. Following your heart does not mean pleasing! It means knowing what is right and doing it in spite of the pull on your emotions. Emotions and heart are not the same. Third, you are here, as we have told you, to tell the Truth. You cannot do that by masking your true needs and feelings and calling it love. We know this is hard and that is why we are made available to you.

Can you show me a way to recognize what the real Truth is? I think I know it but you tell me I am unaware—or unseeing.

You teach the answer to this. It is in the body. If you answer a question, "No, it really doesn't matter," and your body shows you a symptom that says it *does* matter, you must listen. When you try to change how you are, your personality, or the way you think in order to be more pleasing, you have placed yourself where you will not know yourself. Each of you is created differently, for good reason. If you were all to be the same, you would have noticed this. Unfortunately, the society you inhabit prizes image above Truth. This puts a burden on those created for truth telling. Remember Cassandra. All she did was tell the Truth, to prophesy, and for generations to be a depressing figure was to be a Cassandra. But she was true to herself, even though others didn't listen. This is a lesson to learn. She fulfilled her purpose. It was others who did not.

It hurts to hurt others.

And so should you hurt yourself? Does this make sense to you, Beloved? All are precious, and that includes you. Each must do their work and accept the consequences. You are not responsible for happiness. The work you will do, when you have accepted your purpose, will create well-being for so many more than you worry about now. You must trust that this is true. You hurt others in the big picture when you are not truthful about your place in their lives. They must know who you truly are. If they choose to remove themselves from your life, this is not yours to control. Now go to sleep and dream. Be kind to yourself. We will wait until you are ready.

Dialogue XVI

My daughter, are you listening? It feels as though there have been dark veils between us. Are you ready to resume your real work?

I'm ready, and so sorry for my absence…illness, creating a new web site, moving…

There are no right or wrong times for me to come to you. Those other things are illusions—you can change them at any time. You are the power in your own life, the choice-maker.

Why would I choose illness and pain?

Perhaps because it frees you to rest from all your self-imposed busyness. Let it be easy.

I feel the urge to argue, to explain myself.

So be it. But you could use that energy in more productive ways. The world needs you now—unencumbered by doubt, bitterness, false busyness, and unnecessary business. You've done the work. You are ready.

Who speaks to me?

We are your council. We are made up of many. You feel us from time to time, especially when you are teaching, but you have not opened fully to our guidance.

How do I do that?

Take time daily. Sit and listen. When you are in an empty but aware space, you will feel us. We have been with you from the beginning.

I look for you, but I'm tired and fearful of not being supported.

We are your support. Accept that and fear will lift like fog from water.

I am filled with relief—a lightness of being even in my illness.

Your power is the power of God within and without. You never have to fear or want...simply be and follow your soul's direction. We are your soul "mates" as you would call us. Our work is together. No one is alone, unless he chooses to be. Then, his perception will say "I am alone." This is not true, but the person's choice of truth. We will not force our presence on anyone. We must be asked, as you have asked. Now it is time to return to your work. Write The Promise *and then the rest will be clear.*

I am grateful. My heart is full with gratitude for your presence. I will not fear. I am open. I am listening.

We are grateful. Without your voice we are not heard. Tell us to the world. I am known as Jeremiel. Others will reveal themselves in time. Today, I have chosen to come.

Is there anything else?

Love the one you call Lance. He is of us.

He struggles so—illness is with him constantly.

It is not easy to be an earth-bound messenger. Being back in the body is hard. He will do what he was sent for. He will heal many. When you are both well, begin anew with a bigger vision. Anything is possible. Disengage from drama; engage with power.

I get up from bed and take out my deck of angel cards. I hold the deck to my heart for confirmation that what I heard was truly guidance from my soul circle. I shuffle the cards and begin to draw the top card. I hear a definite no. I touch the back of the next card down. Again, a no—and so on through the next six cards. I feel like turning one over and hear, "Not this one, the next one." I draw that card, turn it over, and I see *Jeremiel.* The name of the card is "Overcoming Difficulties." The message reads, "The worst is now behind you, and you are surmounting any previous challenges."

Lance and I leave for Chicago for a week of healing work with Jean Houston. It is mind-bending, life-changing work. At one ceremony, in the church, I see Michael again. We are listening to a harpist and the familiar golden light envelops me. Warm gratitude, unfathomable love, and a giddy kind of joy enter my body. I don't hear his voice, but an energetic presence communicates with me. He tells me that the wound I carry is not a hole that can't be filled and it is not grief. It is a portal to other dimensions and a place where healing takes place. He tells me I can go there anytime. The music stops and we leave the church for our evening session. I go to bed that night determined to talk to Michael when I get home, to ask him to help me heal.

Conversation with Michael after Chicago

"My sweet son, it was a gift of immense loving to feel you with me again, in the Church of the Holy Word. My whole mother-self saw and felt your golden radiance and your blessings. You told me the wound I carried was a portal to healing. I am in need of that healing, and I ask you to accompany me into that place. I'm afraid to go alone. Are you willing? I'm so tired. I need to sleep. Please come in my dreams so I can see you, and you can help me ask for healing. You blessed the union of Lance and me. Bless the whole health of my body. I miss you!"

Lance and I lay face to face—hands on each other's hearts. He believes I can go to Michael. He says, "Go through familiar beautiful music."

I hear Michael's voice. "You have to come alone."

I see our hearts, Lance's and mine, and am so sad. They are scarred and lumpy. Then, light fills them and they begin to heal. We lay quietly for a few minutes. Lance leaves me—I have to go alone.

I begin to fall into a light sleep. I am on a bus. Behind me someone calls out, "What time is it?" I look at my bedside clock (real) and say, "It's 12:16."

"Time to go," Michael's voice says.

I hear Lance call me from the other room, but I have to leave. I slide through and am carried on waves of energy—like rollers. It is light, soothing, and incredibly peaceful—but I can't stay. I hear "equal to all the time you need," which is Jean's mantra, and I am back. I look at the clock. It's 12:30. The room is full of the smell of flowers, and I fall asleep.

It is the beginning of my healing. The next morning, fluid is leaving my body and my blood sugar is down thirty points. The pain in my leg, a constant throb since Chicago, is gone. I begin my morning meditation.

Thank you, whoever has led me through this door. I will remember that I am always safe. The flow of the book has been interrupted and I don't know why. I can only ask that I be open to your voices, any voices that wish to come through me. We are a gray people, saddened by death. Darkness is spreading over our land and the light is like sun behind smog. We need wisdom. I will be patient. I know you have more to tell me.

My Beloved child, you need rest. We will return to you when you are stronger and ready for our next teaching. Do not mourn our absence—we are sending our strength and healing. Be patient.

Dialogue XVII

We have given you time to rest and heal. Now it is time to fulfill your promise.

There are two sides to The Promise: One you were given. One you made. This is about the one you made before you were born. You promised to tell about what happened. You promised to help change the results.

What happened when?

When the Grail replaced the Cauldron; when Woman was denied her true place; when the lies were told; when the Sacred Feminine was buried under the profane masculine. You have been led to this place your whole life. When the nuns said you were blasphemous. When your family said you were too serious, too concerned with the right and wrong of it. When your husband said, "Why can't you just let things be?" Always, you knew about the Soul, the huge wound in woman's Soul.

For the land to be green again, the wound must be healed. The Fisher King, the focus of the Knights, was not wounded in battle. The Fisher King's wound, as we have already told you, was a symbol, used by your writers of all times who have seen and warned your world of the danger. The wound is the *Sacred Feminine sacrificed to war and greed.* You fear

80

the task because it is large, but you are not the only one called. Others are working now. You will find each other. But for now, you must begin. Only in this way will you heal your own body and Soul and the Soul of the planet.

How do I begin?

You have been given help. You have received the gifts of compassion, curiosity, ritual, courage, and writing. There is nothing left but the doing. We are all here. Call on us anytime you are in need. We are your council. You saw us in your dream and you saw us in your past life journey with your mate when you received the book. The time of gravest danger for your planet is here and now. This is your calling. The Sacred Feminine must be restored.

And what about the Promise made to me?

You have the power, through energy, to go to any dimension and realize help and healing; manifest work and prosperity; create music and art; realize understanding. The people of your planet often live lives of *unconscious inattention.* Always you are being guided without knowing it is so. This is not about blaming—you must be clear about that! This is about healing and honoring. The wound cannot be healed unless it is recognized and blessed. That is the truth about all wounding. You must look, see, honor, and it will be healed. This is true of everything.

Song of Greening

Sing the earth into green,
for it has been dry too long.
Sing scarlet for poppies,
dancing toward lion-colored
hills like red umbrellas.
Sing lavender fields;
smell notes rising. Sing
with the lark; laugh
at your presumption, but
sing anyway. It is all

part of the Great Work,
this singing. Is your throat
dry like Mother Earth? Begin
small; try a warble—even
a croak. A frog sings in its
frog way. Soon you will hear
praise pour from your throat
like honeyed wine. It will
surprise you with its joy.
Released from caged silence,
notes will fall upward, seed
the highest clouds, drop back
to Earth—water music.

Part Three:

THE PROMISE

❧

The day's blow
rang out, metallic—or it was I, a bell awakened...
—Denise Levertov, "Variation on a Theme by Rilke"

❧

Dialogue XVIII

Why do you call me to write about women, the struggles of women, the injustices and dishonoring of women? This is in my thoughts and dreams and has been for such a long time. It became a cause for the demise of my marriage. You have taught me about love. Shouldn't we just move forward?

We do this for a good reason. You write and teach about the Sacred Feminine. The first step for women is to clear the old, thus the anger and sadness, in order to create space. This space, this whole cosmos of space, will be filled with honor, love, compassion, and empathy toward all females back to the beginning of time. Then all males will also be free to exist in a loving space. It will be a choice for each one, and you are to make a clear picture; outline a process by which this can happen.

Will you help me? It feels like a huge task. I am humbled before it, and somehow fearful.

Of course we are here to help. That is what we do. Your fear is not founded in reality. You have been chosen.

Chosen. It is a humbling word. Choosing is a word I like: I choose. You choose. Being chosen is a different experience entirely. Once accepted, there is no going back. It is as the poem by Denise Levertov says. I have been struck. I can and I will begin my task and fulfill my promise. I can be nothing less than a bell awakened. The truth has come down to me in my cellular structure, as surely as my great-grandmother granted me her blue eyes. Genetic memory is a scientific fact, an explanation for knowing things that cause us to look at ourselves in astonishment and say, "How did I know that?"

That women of our time must give honor and peace to women who came before us is a certainty in my mind, heart, and soul. Only then can we reclaim our true soul selves, meet men on a balanced level, and thus balance the earth. Can we do this before it is too late? The instructors I see and hear would not be wasting their time if the task were not ours to do. We must begin, however, or it *will* be too late.

Ancestor

As far back
as the heart's eye
casts, they wait for words
of love, honor, appreciation,
and great empathy. Pass bouquets
of rosemary and orchids to hands
empty of all but hope. Warm
grandmothers tending the fire of family
lying cold and awake behind the door.
Go down the steps of the past, touching
the shoulder of a mother as she adds
meat to the pot, flax to the spool.
See her eyes lift from her task?
A shiver runs across her back
as she feels your presence,
accepts your blessing,
takes heart.

I light sage, play music, and access my higher self in meditation, praying myself back in time using Sacred Feminine Imaging. (I will teach you this work in the last section.) I ask the women of my family line and all women of the past to tell me what it is they need. I close my eyes, breathe deeply, and wait to be told as I watch time fly beneath me.

This is what happened when I stopped and drifted down into a time past. Intuition told me who was there.

My maternal great-great-great-grandmother stands surrounded by huge trees—trees so numerous there is barely room for her and a few others in the clearing. I know without doubt that she is a healer and a leader of ritual. I watch as the women begin moving around a banked fire, chanting a deep, melodious sound. One woman comes forward, baring her arm. There is a huge wound, clean and pink where new skin is growing. My forebear sniffs the arm, puts salve on the wound, and wraps it with a rough but clean cloth. She looks satisfied. Another woman throws herbs into the flames, and sparks fly upward, dying as they reach the canopy of dark green overhead. The forest grows thicker and quieter, as if holding its breath. The clearing vibrates, pregnant with expectation, but the women are not afraid. They are there for a purpose. I lean closer and place my hand on the back of my mother's relative, wishing her a blessed life. She is startled and shivers, pulling her shawl closer around her. She looks behind her, smiles directly into my eyes, and nods. It was a good thing that just happened; the future has honored the past. She turns back toward the fire, where three young girls in long red dresses have just appeared in the crowded space. I feel myself being drawn away, unable to stay as one generation begins the teaching of another.

When I finish my meditation, I think about this woman. Was she safe? Or did they call what she did witchcraft and punish her for it? I feel a shiver as I remember a recent look at the city of Salem's *City Guide*. The web site shows a 1990s memorial to the women who were murdered during the last of the witch trials. The poignant words of Elizabeth Howe, hung on July 19, 1692, will be with me forever. "If it was the last moment I was to live, God knows I am innocent…"

I would never know, but I am certain that, back through time, this woman at the fire felt me thanking her for who she was, honoring her for what she did. What was it, exactly, that I was supposed to learn in this process? I believe it was clear that I saw women who honored their inner wisdom and were honored for it. It is, as I already knew, part of my path to share that honoring with others, to help them reclaim the sacred heritage. When I'm told to *forget about it*, I will remember her. I wish I had asked her name! I think about her love for healing and ritual. Maybe this is where I received it.

She Who Knows

Behind my eyes, she tells me stories
of my sadness, haunting loss going
back thousands, tens of thousands,
of years; lifetimes spent learning,
teaching, and healing.
My body settles to the ground
in a long-remembered folding of legs,
arms. The hair of my head begins to
grow in length and weight, my skin
changes to the color of Sedona rock.
A melody rises in my mouth, cold
like white water in Oak Creek
touched by smooth stones, and I
remember what I know. I walked
these cliffs and canyons, stepped
softly on Mother Earth, lifted my face
to Father Sun, full of gratitude
and blessing. When the rains came,
the floor of the canyon bloomed.
I was faint with the heady scent of
Earth's perfume. Sage smoke, essence
of ceremony, rose and none doubted
woman's wisdom. Gone now, that time
and place. Women mourn its passing,
memory stirring like bear after a long
winter, bringing tears and no explaining.

With that song, that chant arising
from nowhere, we are surprised in our
modern guises and bow our heads.
We are in the presence of Mother,
She Who Knows.

In Dialogue XVII, the words were: "when the Grail replaced the cauldron." After reading about this, I understand where the great lie began. Scholars know the meaning of the cauldron, which is why the search for the Grail has been relegated to fiction and adventure, not meant for truth. The Cauldron was the image of the goddess. All over the world, the people worshipped at places where life bubbled from the earth, the sign of the presence of the feminine. These places had the names of the goddess in all her manifestations, including the baths at Bath, England, sacred to the Goddess Sulis, where pilgrims went for thousands of years before it became a Christian site. In the Middle Ages, the cauldron was worshipped in the same way as the male symbol of the cross.

One truth is always available in stories of the Grail. The world has gone gray, the king is wounded, and the people are in mourning, looking for answers. Universally, this is the denial of the sacred feminine. The world has a soul just as each person has a soul. Individually, when the truth of the soul is denied—in other words, we have not kept our promise—there will be no joy, no color. Without purpose, there is no passion. Each person is mourning the loss of their own joy, their own purpose. The world today is in just that place of sadness and grayness. We would know it if we lifted our heads from our computers and televisions and really looked.

It is a lifetime of study to go into all the places where the early beliefs were rewritten to conform to the beginning of patriarchal religion and civilization. The damage was done out of fear that the people would not listen to the voices of men if they still consulted the instincts of the feminine. For our purposes, it is enough to know that the search for the cauldron of the goddess, the long buried healing of the feminine, was changed into male knights searching for the vessel that held the wine at the Last Supper of Jesus. It is only by reawakening the feminine—the healing, receptive, nurturing—that we can find our way back to truth. The liquid we seek is the water of forgiveness and healing which flows from the heart of the feminine, and the blood of regeneration and birth that flows from the body of the feminine.

I have felt the tension all my life of three separate pulls:

- The pull of the Sacred that led me to the convent at thirteen.
- The pull of the intellectual that led me to books, teachers, and study.
- The pull of the sensual/sacred body that led me to marriage, children, and sexual love.

How I would love to talk to my ancestor! How did she balance all of that in her day, with a life span one third as long as mine? I see her practicing her spiritual life, and I know that was the process of study under some woman who came before her.

There are women in my workshops who say, "I have done nothing with my life. I've raised my kids, and now I take care of my grand-kids." As I continue to ask them about their lives, they reveal the depths of knowing based on their meditation practice, recipes, child behavior, household accounting, and negotiations with husband, child, and community. They are a treasure trove of knowledge and don't even know it. If they haven't followed the linear instructional path of *do this, then this, then this,* they think they haven't accomplished anything.

Now, in the brilliant later years that resemble the leaves of fall, I ask that we honor the accumulated wisdom of ourselves and others. Those who have been brainwashed out of their circular knowledge into the linear learning pushed at them from society are ready to move back into the circle. Too few of us honor them. The time has come to do so. It is part of the promise I made long ago without knowing.

As I begin this morning's work, I think about how hard it is for women to separate themselves from responsibility. We are chosen to do a larger work, particularly later in life, but we have established ourselves as *she who can be depended upon.* To practice saying no is wrenching as we seek to establish a new life for ourselves, one that fulfills *our* needs as much as the needs of others. Frequently, our new work will involve helping others, but the in-between time must be all about us. I meditated about this for a week every night before sleep, and the following is only one of the dreams I had that showed my insecurity about giving up my responsibilities.

I share a home with three other women. They are Iraqi. All the houses on this street are connected. A bomb drops a block away. People are milling in the square below me. I'm on the balcony and know if they see me they will come to the door. I know that I can help or I can lock the door. I lock the door. One of my house mates returns, I let her in and relock the door.

In scene two, I am driving past wrecks, and I don't stop. A man is lying in the intersection. Someone else stops to help him. I don't stop.

I have several other similar scenes, including one with my grandson. In these dreams, I feel shame every time I don't help. A council of voices, compassionate though they may sound, tells me that if I revert to caretaking I won't be doing what I'm meant to do. I return to the earlier instructions from those who guide me. In Dialogue XVI, I was told in no uncertain terms that it was time to fulfill my promise, my commitment to taking the wounding of women's souls into my work and my daily activities. This is not a small thing. The Sacred Feminine resides in all of us and *must* be recognized for the world to heal herself in all areas, including our individual relationships and the relationships of countries and the relationship of the Universe to each of us.

Men and children will benefit as men are relieved of the perceived instructions of the masculine and have time to tune in to their creative and nurturing natures. Some have already discovered the joy of this, but the culture does not honor their choices. It is time for me to tell another truth, and this one is bigger than my own personal truth. I will be aware and attuned to the truth of my ancestors, and I will encourage others to do the same through my writing, my workshops, and my life. *This is my Promise.*

෴

*I swear the earth shall surely be complete to him or
her who shall be complete,
The earth remains jagged and broken only to him
or her who remains jagged and broken.*

—Walt Whitman

෴

Is it necessary to go into all of the suffering of women, and thus families and children, through the ages? Is it possible that we don't already know about the intentional death of the goddess? Is it necessary to go into detail about the Inquisition and the Witch Hunts and the millions of innocent women, usually healers, who were murdered? Must I chronicle the lives of the women who were hanged, drowned, raped, or burned because they dared to learn to read or write?

Historians have written of these things throughout time, though they are not seen by most students. In my workshops I say the numbers killed during the Inquisition/Witch Hunts, and women don't believe it. "We would know," they say to me. Until they look it up themselves, the millions who died are not real. I believe what I am being asked to do is to redress this history by honoring those who lived it, creating ritual and work that honors them, and naming it the biggest wound, or holocaust if you will, ever suffered in the body of humankind and the earth. Every time a person, man or woman, goes against the feminine knowing within themselves to create a situation of harm, either to other persons or the planet, they are enlarging the wound. As I finish a day's work and fall asleep, I have a final dream on the subject of responsibility and guilt.

I am driving down a dirt road in the country, past barbed wire fences, pastoral scenes of great serenity and beauty. I see her, and I am stunned—a grand and glorious cow towers behind a fence. She is red and white with long, graceful legs and a huge, white suede-like udder that sways heavily as she moves toward me. I see a herd of horned steer coming toward her, and know she is in grave danger. I call to her to step over the fence—it is no barrier to her, but will stop her pursuers. She looks at me with sad longing, and I watch in horror as she is surrounded and eventually disappears beneath the herd. I cry out, wail to heaven that she could have just stepped over the fence. Why didn't she save herself? What could I have done?

I know this dream is profoundly important to me. In the morning I research, discovering that the cow is the ancient symbol of the feminine, also known as The Great Mother. She is the familiar symbol of Isis, procreation, and maternal instincts. The Celts saw her as the Celestial Cow, red with white ears, representing the Yin principle and the earth.

I feel, instinctively, that this cow represents the strength of the feminine that has been fenced in by expectations and rules, and the danger is real. Unless the female within regains her sense of strength and purpose, she will finally die beneath the demands of those individuals who simply use her up. She is asking me to help her. This I can't refuse to do. This was one plea I was not being told to ignore.

⁓

Children say that people are hanged sometimes
for speaking the truth.
—Joan of Arc, words at her trial, February 23, 1431

⁓

In the Dialogues, I was told of my power, the promise made to me. This included going to other dimensions for information, healing, and comfort. It is part of my Truth that I have done and continue to do this. I give you an example.

During the work with Jean Houston, I learned to go to the deep stillness that is necessary to access all the information that we are given. It was not easy for me to still my questioning mind long enough to hear answers. Jean spoke of Parmenides, the Priest of Apollo, who taught others to "travel to the deep; see loaded coded dreams."

"Deep stillness," she instructed, "is necessary. At the still point of the turning world, the stillness carries us into a reality we've never known— deep space and time—utter stillness."

On this day, we entered an exercise I call "The Gate." As we prepared to go down into the underworld, I felt a strong fear. Any visualization that led me beneath the earth, or, symbolically, into my darkest self, was a challenge for me—one that I usually failed. Always, the fate of Inanna, or Ishtar, reared its head, and I saw her hanging, dead meat on a hook in the underworld. Death by an untimely burial was a nightmare I had for years after reading "Fall of the House of Usher," by Edgar Allan Poe. However, Jean told us to leave a protector at the gate who would bring us home, no matter what happened. I gratefully visualized my three daughters, tripling my chances of rescue. Then, following the guidance of Jean, I entered through the gates of the Underworld. She would leave us to our own devices as soon as we entered the carriage of the daughters of the Sun.

The daughters of the Sun await, their carriage drawn by a white mare. I join them, my insides shaking violently, and we descend down a winding road paved with black marble. It becomes a spiral and winds down, down, down into blackness, into the place of fear. The carriage comes to a stop. In a halo of gold, I see the beautiful daughters of light motion to me to step out, and as I do, they disappear. A man stands quietly by a huge building; he wears a garment of white with a vivid green square below the neck and a sash around his waist. He is expecting me. Silently, I follow him through massive doors into an echoing hall, the size of a football stadium.

Throughout the hall are sections of shimmering color. I look more closely, and I see they are vials hanging from a ceiling that arches high above the hall. The vials are glass, like the vials that hold ammonia and can be broken open under your nose when you faint. In this case, the vials are about twenty feet long, from the ceiling to near the floor, and are as big around as a fist. They are vibrating, their different tones creating a beautiful harmonic humming throughout the building. Each vial has colored liquid in both ends, a crystal liquid that shimmers with the vibration. Each color is gathered in its own space: violet with violet, red with red, etc. I see that each section has its own healing vibration, property, tone, and color. I ask the teacher for healing, and he leads me to the back of the hall. He tells me that in each section I am to grasp two vials, one with each hand, and I will know for which area of my body they are meant.

I begin with the lowest tone, which vibrates in my legs. The color is a vibrant Florida sky blue. The vials fit perfectly in my hands, as if they are made for me. Next, I move to the mid-tone vials, which are gold in color and vibrate in my reproductive, sexual, and digestive organs. The next higher tone, vibrating in my heart, is a lighter yellow, like pale tulips. As before, I hold the vials and they caress my palms, fitting perfectly as my fingers curl around. Finally, I move to the area of highest vibration. I stand, holding the vials, an effervescent silver/white vibrating through my arms, into my heart, and out my head. Healing flows through me like shimmering water. I leave my body and am high above the building, even though I am below the earth—a gift of traveling beyond the norm. Looking down, I see that the vials are part of a huge system that resembles a pipe organ—it is a pipe organ. The music is stunning and fills me with joy. I return, reluctantly, to the inside of the organ and my body.

The teacher leads me out through the door of the building where another teacher awaits.

He is The Prophet. "The world will only change if you and others recognize no borders and no boundaries—only life. Each life and type of life is equal in value."

He passes me on to the next teacher.

He is The Poet. "Speak your words: they will heal."

And the next, the Law Giver. "The laws of nations must respect all peoples and their needs."

And, lastly, the Healer. "Only through your work will you heal. Only through right-doing will you heal."

Softly, I'm wrapped in an all-encompassing light, so compassionate, so "Mother," that I don't want to leave. I want to stay here, in this light, forever. Then I realize why I left all three of my daughters at the gate. I need their strength and purpose to bring me home to complete my work.

As these beautiful women lift me on their love, I arrive back in the room, back in my body, and totally shaken by this profound imagistic journey. The teachings are Universal, but somehow personal. I feel the heart of me responding.

Fully rejoining the room, I become aware of a group of women nearby talking about *regular stuff,* like movies and makeup, and I feel irritation rising in me. After all, look where we have been! And then I had to smile at my Aquarius-like love for everything on the cosmic level disintegrating on the personal level. Each person makes their own choice. Theirs is not my business; only my choices are my business. If my choice is to expose the dangers of the loss of the feminine, I can do that without judging those who are making other choices.

That is my challenge—therein lies my wound. To live the mythic/mystic life in the ordinary world is a holy task, but with this kind of assistance and this level of knowing, we can do it, at least one minute at a time. Our wounding keeps us from moving into our purpose, whatever that may be. But we have nothing to fear! We are simply and naturally going into the life we were meant to live. The proof of this knowing is too overwhelming to ignore.

It's not that we didn't notice things were not as they should be. In the 1950s and 1960s, "mother's little helpers," immortalized by the Rolling Stones, got many women through the day, while Valium could be found in the purses of most of my friends. Some of the women who gathered in my kitchen in the late afternoons, children beneath their feet, were already on their first cocktails. What were we covering up in our lives? What pain or lack in our soul was trying to get our attention?

Today, it has gotten worse. Overall unhappiness is palpable in our world. For example, when we medicate ourselves because we are asking, "Is that all there is?" in the midst of wealth and comfort; when we see our children failing in their lives and their health in the midst of the most affluence our country has ever known; when more children than we can count are medicated so they can survive in the school environment; when we see couples divided by a gulf so great they need to yell to hear each other; when our families are in chaos and only 30 percent of married couples take more than 20 minutes for love-making—on an infrequent basis; when we see child abuse of all forms increasing; when sexual abuse touches over 50 percent of girls and boys in their own families; when people build 30,000-square-feet houses to store their toys; when we see that chaos escalate to countries destroying each other because they named themselves *other*. There is no need to go on. You know it, in your heart of hearts, or you wouldn't be reading this book.

Looking straight at the Truth is only the prelude to a cure, but it is the beginning. We are being asked to uncover the Truth to save ourselves and our planet. There is a minimum requirement here. Honor the past in the form of our ancestors; honor the present in the form of ourselves, our families, and our communities; and honor the future by providing a planet where the children who are yet to come can breathe, run, play, and prosper in their bodies and spirits. And it is to be done in love and gratitude. It is a sacred charge, not a job. All people of good heart are hearing the call at this time. We ignore it at our own peril—the peril of our planet and our souls. It is too big to ignore and too sacred to take lightly.

I have two sons who are generous and gentle—one an aware, caretaking father and husband, totally involved in the lives of his children; the other a musician, writer, contractor, Renaissance man who stands up to be counted when he sees injustice. They are serving the Truth in their own way. My partner, Lance, is as committed to the resurrection of the strengths of the feminine as I am. It is only because the feminine qualities have been damaged that women are called to do the greatest work within. Walking with men of compassion and understanding is a gift. There are many of us walking and flying with you. Have courage.

Angel, look away.
I cannot afford to yield the last defense,
to go back.
'Not back, but deeper'
said the angel, folding his wings
to wait.

—May Sarton, *"The Fear of Angels"*

We are not the first to be called, "Not back, but deeper." You are asking too much of me, this amazing poet seems to be saying down the years. When we are called by our highest knowing, our guides or angels, it is sometimes too terrifying to face.

At this point, old learned habits of fear are what stand between me and my work. Too much energy has been wasted on the age-old questions of women. What will people think? Will I be liked? Am I willing to take on the judgment of others and still be comfortable? Will my family suffer from my outspokenness? Those questions seem petty and unbelievably dated in the face of all I have been learning, and yet they governed a large part of my life, as they continue to govern huge numbers of women. For me, it was time to move on. In the meantime, I had more to learn.

I was training to be certified as a Time Dimension Therapist. With my work taking on new dimensions, I am called to take on a larger field of being. How to do that? First of all, by recognizing that there is more to us than what we see on a one-dimensional level, and certainly more than we have been taught to see. We have the ability to access many dimensions and see the truth of our abilities. This is not to be taken lightly, because once seen we cannot pretend to have *not* seen. According to the latest scientific findings in physics and biology, variations of me may exist on many timelines: before, parallel, here, and after. I have the ability to jump the timelines and change who and what I am. I can plant my intentions *up* the timeline and watch it happen. I can return to the past and honor those women who have suffered and passed along to us our greatest gifts. Some of this is incorporated in my work, the rest is for others to contemplate, study, and write about.

We can also access the place where women of the past honored in themselves only that which was masculine. Is it any wonder this is so? If women had to wear pants and change their names in order to do their work—Joan of Arc and George Sand are examples—how understandable that they were absorbing even more intolerance toward their fellow women. George Sand, recognized as a feminist and trail blazer, had very little positive to say about women. Her way of complimenting herself was to say she was more like a man than a woman. "You believe in the grandeur of women…" she wrote Charlotte Marliani in 1839. "Having been more demoralized, it's inevitable that women have the mentality of slaves." Later, she wrote, "Equality will always be an exception. I therefore prefer men to women, and I say this without malice, seriously convinced that the goals of nature are logical and complete."

This attitude of women toward women modifies as they age, even in the case of George Sand, but the damage has been done. We are still absorbing the message of inferiority of the feminine, the huge energetic mass of past and present thought that says women are "other." The Chinese government sanctions mass adoption of their "useless" girl children, other societies continue the process of genital mutilation, and American girls flock to web sites that assist them in becoming Anorexic or Bulimic. Local newspapers aimed at the hip and chic are filled with slick ads for the latest plastic surgery or poison injections. And then there is Disney!

I have been criticized for my take on the fairy tales as they are presented by Disney. There have been a few exceptions lately, but most of us grew up mooning over Cinderella or Snow White. "Someday my prince will come!" Much has been written in feminist literature about the inside out readings of the fairy tales and how they were presented to women in the 1940s, 1950s, and beyond. Those who are interested in more can find many books on the subject. I will present you with an example I use in my workshops so that we understand the damage done and the healing that is needed.

All of the old stories were an oral tradition that taught people the ways of the world, the ways society expected moral behavior, and lessons about our interior search for our own good and our shadow side. Cinderella was no exception. In her world, the stepsisters and stepmother were very beautiful, and so was she. (Contrast that to Disney, where good is beautiful and bad is ugly. Usually, the villain is female *and* evil *and* ugly; witness Snow White's stepmother as the hag, Cinderella's stepmother, and the nemesis of the Little Mermaid.)

In the original story, the stepsisters were beautiful, gorgeously dressed, and coiffed, but had no soul. Cinderella had beauty and a soul, which they didn't recognize. The beauty they covered in ashes so she would not be seen by anyone else either. A soul is a fearsome thing to those who wish to dominate. But the Prince "saw" her, soul and all.

When their turn came, the sisters cut off pieces of their feet to fit into the slipper—a warning of what we lose when we conspire to win at any price. At the end of the story, as the Prince's page asks if any other females live in the house, Cinderella's father denies there is anyone else in the house but the serving girl. The Prince asks to see her, since the edict read *all* maidens. Unlike Disney's version, where she appears, miraculously, in the clothes she wore to the ball, Cinderella comes from the fireplace, ashes and all. The Prince slips on the shoe, recognizes her spirit and soul beneath the ashes, and honors her with his love.

Cinderella, being a kind and generous woman, finds grooms for her stepsisters. However, they have not learned the ways of soul. As they ride in the wedding procession, they are thrilled because they will at least be *near* power. (Read this as looking forward to feasting on Cinderella's energy.) According to the earliest versions of the story, ravens descend on the procession and peck out the stepsister's eyes, signaling that they have not yet seen Truth. They did not grow, so they must now suffer in darkness until they "see the light." Sometimes it is only in darkness that we can see inside and discover our true essence.

Today's parents judge the stories too bloody and harsh for their children, and yet television, movies, and video games are bathed in violence for no good reason. Children's books have taken on a dark and treacherous side. It's not hard to find the moral in this story, or others like it. In our time, the moral is quite different. Thanks to the Disney version, Cinderella perseveres with the help of magic, but she only wins through being more beautiful than the other women and then she goes on to live "happily ever after." In spite of writings to the contrary, we are not out of the woods. We have simply changed locations.

A recent article in *Forbes*—yes, I said *Forbes*—magazine was headlined "Don't Marry a Woman with a Career."

"The more successful she is the more likely she is to grow dissatisfied with you," the author writes. It didn't take long for women across America to find his article insulting and idiotic, but also amazingly short-sighted. With 70 percent of women working, what kind of gene pool does that leave for his readers? That he could even get such idiocy published today, let alone in a serious business magazine, says that there is a lot of work to be done.

Helen Fisher, an anthropologist at Rugers University, told *Good Morning America* she was "…surprised that the man thinks it, astonished that he wrote it. And I'm astonished that anyone published it, particularly *Forbes*." (From an article by Nancy Weiner, ABCnews.com)

My only disagreement with Ms. Fisher is that I'm not surprised that he thinks it. Through an understanding of the years of indoctrination of men and women into the frailties of women, sometimes at their mother's knee, we can learn to empathize and then forgive. But it is important, first, to count the ways the feminine is desecrated, look them in the face, and stop the process. We can redefine the description of women and replace the "other" description, but only by acknowledging the energy that went into creating this huge thought of inferiority.

Today's media assault on young women shows us that this dormant indoctrination has been awakened and we are, again, in a position to see past, present, and future as a continuum of certain energetic behaviors and beliefs. Talented young women who desire fame, especially in the music business, are pressured to present the whore persona as opposed to the heroine we see in the original Cinderella. How much easier this is than the years of work and attention required to become a fully spiritual human woman. It simply requires tons of makeup, clothes that defy the title, bodies starved to size 0, and in some, artificially pumped up lips and breasts.

I saw a picture of Nicole Richie on the cover of a magazine in the grocery store. If it was not doctored, the eighty pound woman would have qualified for the cover of a magazine asking for aid for a victim of famine. In a day when the species is larger then ever, women are shrinking themselves to zeros, literally. What would it mean to be a zero? We don't have to spend a lot of brain power answering that question. We all know what a zero equals: nothing. A woman looking in the mirror saying *I am beautiful, I am a zero*, has denied her power, her energetic presence, and her true beauty.

Now that we have the perfect look for a recording star, we move on to talent. Some are truly talented, but since voices can be simulated or beefed up in the studio, that's the last thing on the list. We've all seen a natural talent reduced to that voice you can't put a name to. Unique natural women legends like Tina Turner and Bonnie Raitt would not even get a foot in the door today, though Tina does have the shoes.

In the August 2006 *Rolling Stone* magazine, Bob Dylan is interviewed. He bemoans the fact that the quality of recording has disintegrated over the years to the point where he doesn't even like his own CDs. He seems to have missed the style over substance memo. And who is setting the style for today's teens and pre-teens? Schlock purveyors who like the bottom line better than music.

In the 1960s and 1970s, the energy of women surging into the workplace and feminist thought combined to create a possibility of a free-thinking woman. This scared a lot of people who had a vested interest in women needing their guidance. Thanks to the pendulum swinging back to ownership of the feminine by the media message, only the clothes women are wearing have changed. The whore model seems to have replaced the CEO model at places as sacred as Macy's. These once underground clothes proliferate in the population of young girls, thanks to the linkage of department stores, designers, and ad companies. They are also appealing to their mothers, so the girls have to go one step further to differentiate themselves from the last generation. Body decoration bloomed on teens and then we started to see cleavage tattoos on moms at the grocery store. Oops. What do we do next to prove we are *not mom*? Nose studs, tongue piercing, and half-shaved heads? Hopefully, that did it for now.

We need to think about this in an emotional as well as social context. When I see the outlandish lengths teens are forced to go in order to differentiate from their parents, it's an amazing awakening. What are they to do when mom buys her clothes in the teen department, or dresses in a designer knock-off of clothes kids invented for riding skateboards? Fear of aging is only one of the things in operation here. Instead of mentoring, we are hiding out in youth as long as possible. We have somehow been taught that we have no place in life as role models unless we look like "Desperate Housewives." This is a great loss for our daughters, and sons, who need strong feminine role models, not Stepford Wives.

It is also true that the heels of shoes go higher as attention to the inner work declines. When models begin to stumble and fall on the runways, as happened recently, will we understand that we are being asked to balance too much on the soles (souls) of our feet? The essence of spiritual meditation is connection to the earth, especially through the feet. Added to the concrete that keeps us from connecting is three inches or more of leather-covered metal rod and intense pain in the arches. What are we thinking?

Many things have changed above ground, but in the subterranean caverns of the body and the body politic, much is the same. We are not fooled when cars are named for the soul and finding your own path—or are we?

The possibilities are created for me as a teacher and facilitator to help others to find their best selves, recover the feminine side of their lives, and picture what they can accomplish with this realization. In the last part of this book I will share exercises that I use in my workshops and individual sessions to help women access their ancestral memory and use the information to mine the potential of the future.

Marion Woodman, a prominent Jungian analyst, was interviewed for the book *The Feminine Face of God*, by Sherry Anderson and Patricia Hopkins. In the interview, she stated the following:

> One of the problems women have today is that they're not willing to find the river in their own life and surrender to its current. They're not willing to spend time, because they feel they are being selfish. They grow up trying to please other people and they rarely ask themselves, who am I? Rarely. And then life starts to feel meaningless because they live in terms of pleasing, rather than in terms of being who they are.

I believe she is right, but there is more to the puzzle. I go to bed with the question in my mind: Is this only about becoming less of a pleaser?

I dream of my inner healer. She is female, tall, gowned—her long hair wound in a coronet around her head. She shows me how to send healing. I raise my hands as instructed to send the rays of healing, and I see the mothers and children of Iraq. I hear my inner voice tell me what I know already. "Your path is for the women—to release them from the shame of earlier stories and stereotypes, and then to encourage their strength and self-esteem. In this way, they and men will re-find their way to love and healing. In the breaking down is the healing. Wounds are our doorways to our higher truth.

In the morning I tell Lance about my dream. "She reminded me of a picture I saw of Hypatia," I tell him. He remembers when we talked about her. She was a healer, mathematician, and greatly honored woman at the height of Egyptian culture. The head of the Platonist school at Alexandria in about 400 AD, mail came to her simply addressed to "The Philosopher." She was brutally murdered by those who feared the education and the sacred qualities of her work. She was dragged from her classroom into the street by Christians who found her teachings Pagan. There, she was skinned alive with oyster shells. The Golden Age of Alexandria died with her.

She is another memory stored in the cells of women over the ages—another warning to be careful and stay safe. And therein is my answer. Marion Woodman sees us as responding to training, and she is correct. I see us, also, responding to old fears, and I know that no matter how much work we do to be less pliable and more self oriented, we will not be successful without acknowledging the accumulation of our cellular fears.

Feminist studies are linear: this happened, then this, then this, and this was the result. My instincts tell me, as Jill pointed out, we carry the record within us. If that is so, a warning system lets us know when we are about to do something that led to some awful consequences in the past. Without the knowledge of what it is we're feeling, we back off and resume the position.

Some of us carry the burden of that record consciously and are being asked to put it out publicly. The reason is to honor, in a circular, not linear, fashion, those who were dishonored and not spoken about. How is it *possible* that the murder of all those women in history (and certain men of gentle qualities) goes unnoticed in the history books and the psyche of people? Of course it is *mentioned*, but is that enough? *The largest genocide in recorded time was the witch hunt era—the time of the infamous Malleus Maleficarum* where women were accused of cutting off the genitals of men and feeding them to birds. This was the time of the Inquisition. The churchmen who wrote the *Malleus*, the handbook for the Inquisition, wrote: "No one does more harm to the Catholic faith than midwives."

We know, rightly so, about slavery, the murder of the Jews in the camps, and Stalin's death camps. We know some, but not enough, about the more recent genocides in Africa and Eastern Europe. We only "commemorate" the witch hunts—the murder of millions of women—once a year. Think Halloween and cute drawings of wart-covered witches on broomsticks.

The Inquisition's campaign to cut women off from their own direct experience of spiritual vision, or their Goddess-given moral codes, occupies nearly five centuries of European history. About nine million* persons were executed after 1484 and uncounted numbers before that date, mostly women. The executions were carried out with a febrile brutality exceeding that of any other organized persecution ever known, not excepting the Nazi's twentieth-century holocaust... (Barbara G. Walker*, *The Crone*, Harper, San Francisco, 1988)

> Oh, the danger of making others "other." When one side sees itself as virtuous and right, it has almost un-imaginable permission to punish the other side, which is by definition immoral and wrong. Right now, as I write this, hundreds of women in Iraq who were used to going to university, wearing western clothes, and speaking out are being beaten or having their heads shaved, or finally, assassinated for those exact same activities. This is especially rampant in Basra, where the British are in charge. Dr. Kefaya, a woman who worked with women and children in the hospital at the City University, re-fused to stay home. After she was murdered, some of the British officers acknowledged that they "felt uncomfort-able" with the situation, but a spokesman for the For-eign Office would only say the government of Iraq was supportive of the women.

And we, as Americans, don't even approach the subject. What is different here from the silence of any culture when people are being systematically eliminated? Within our culture, women like Eve Ensler are raising awareness of violence against women on a large scale. Her V-Day efforts are heroic. There are others, but coverage by the media

Estimates range from three to nine million, but no count has been done.

is sparse. We are more interested in the latest pairing and unpairing of starlets and rock stars than the brave women of Afghanistan who invite death by lowering their veils and telling us what is happening to them.

As women raise themselves, through amazingly hard work, to positions of power in the media, they have an obligation. I know that this is a statement that stirs anger among some of these women. They fought the fight to get there, they don't want to rock the boat and slide overboard. Oh, how I understand, and my compassion is strong in their favor. But, and this is a big caveat, they have the *power* to bring attention to the huge threat facing all of us, including themselves and their families. This is not a time for self-preservation, but planet preservation. We watch them rise with great pride and we ask for their leadership. Selling us shoes and wardrobes we can't afford is beneath them. They have risen into the rare air that allows them to lead. We are waiting and supportive, and as long as they are in their Truth, they will continue to rise on the thermals of power.

I am not saying all women must stand forth and stand out. I am acknowledging those who have ascended, recently, to the top of the journalism heap. Katie Couric is now a nightly news anchor. Her publicity shot, put out by the network, had been carved into a fantasy figure via computer tampering. The before woman was a lovely woman, and the after woman a size most women can't even imagine. To what purpose?

~~~

Love is a supreme force which the Eternal Consciousness sent down from itself into an obscure and darkened world that it might bring back that world and its beings to the Divine.

—Mira Alfassa, "The Mother's Vision," twentieth-century French mystic

~~~

If we return to the concept of loving versus being enamored of the material world, the darkness will lift. When our energy is fully engaged with the universe, we can acquire the material things that we need for a good life. The difference is in the purpose of the acquiring. I am suggesting that women of high profile could be carriers of this light. Countless women serve this feminine concept of love wherever they work—within families, schools, and non-profit and for-profit organizations and business. My own daughters and sisters do this work through businesses as varied as teaching, building construction, the Law, and nursing. They drop their gentle and compassionate teachings into the pool of their communities and the circles expand into other circles and we are all the better for it.

So, what is the purpose of bringing this all to the forefront now? Because it is time for a resurrection of the Truth as experienced by many women, past and present. This is not meant to be a bleak portrait or a sad reminiscence, but a resurrecting of the meaning of these women's lives, or at least an acknowledgment that honors who they were and are. Speaking out sometimes feels dangerous. If it feels so to me, what about the women of the Middle East? China? Africa? Afghanistan, India, and Pakistan? The macho culture of Mexico that allows women to be abducted and murdered and their underwear displayed in a man's yard like notches on a gun, is sickening. In Juarez, close to the border with Texas, hundreds of women have been raped and murdered, with little consequence to the macho culture that hides the perpetrators. Ginger Thompson of the *New York Times* writes that "...police and other officials have become suspected of links to the crimes" (September 26, 2005). Her articles are from the foreign desk. It needs to be on the front page, not an item to note in a local weekend edition. Where is the outrage? How alone these women must feel—and how truly alone they are. Organizations that try to bring this horror to light find it very difficult to get the press to respond. Why?

Many modern Americans are finding the Buddhist path comforting and loving. I agree, but would like to see the raising up of the women of the countries where Buddhism is practiced. The same is true of Muslim countries. A complete reading of the founders of these religions bears no resemblance to the treatment of women by some practitioners of these religions. The same can be said for many Christian sects where women are slaves to their husbands, brothers, and fathers and chastised for their unclean bodies.

In August of 2006, a Sunday school teacher at a Baptist church in Watertown, New Jersey, was fired for the sin of being female. The minister decided on a literal interpretation of the first Epistle to Timothy: "I do not permit a woman to teach or have authority over a man; she must be silent." Unfortunately, the Reverend Timothy LaBouf is also on the Watertown City Council. What kind of unbiased decisions can we expect of him in that capacity?

The feminine must rise into balance with the masculine on this planet or we are doomed to repeat our mistakes until we are no more. Women cannot do this alone—fortunately we have men of goodwill working alongside us. Some scientists say the end of life as we know it is only a few years away; others give us a generation to work with. Whichever is true, we don't have a lot of time. We must give up the idea that we can just forget the past and move on. We must honor the past, recognize the damage done by therapies that blame "mother" in every case, and forgive those women who judged, and continue to judge, women who make choices that are not the same as ours. Our model can be the Hutu and Tutsi apology rituals: we must look, honor, and ask forgiveness before we return to the family. I will never again be silenced by those who say we are better off to just move on. We cannot do so without acknowledging the past and giving those who were dishonored the honor they deserve.

Prayer at Times of Change

Holy Mother, Blessed woman who sees me
as I am, guide me on this journey of discovery
and love. Break the chains around my heart
with gentle hands and hold me when I cry
for losses long ignored. Cradle me in your love
as I bring forth all that is unworthy and discard
it and again, when I bring forth all that is true
and worthy and bless it. I am grateful for this
opportunity and fearful in my weakest moments
of what I will find and how I will react. Bless
me, remind me of the strength I have been given,

keep me aware of my human errors so I may
correct them in love, and bless them as they go.

I wrote this prayer when I was on retreat before teaching a work-shop for a group of women. I had been dreaming about the feminine in all guises, but had returned to the harbor of my youth, the Blessed Mother. No longer a practicing Catholic, I am drawn daily to the energy surrounding the statue I have of Mary and one of Kwan Yin, Goddess of Compassion, and Isis, a woman of all parts and partner to Osiris in complete devotion and equality. Isis became the touchstone for our company, as she represented a view of the world that my partner and I believe is possible: the triumph of love, the sacred quality of life, and the beauty of serving the earth.

Though these beautiful representations of the Sacred Feminine share my altar, Mary had been missing for many years. As my son lay dying, I had begged for her intercession. I had a bond with this mortal woman who had lost her son, and I knew she knew what I was feeling. My husband's aunt took one of my precious visitation times in the ICU to anoint Michael with water from Lourdes, and I believed the Blessed Mother went into that room with her. At this time in my life, in my thirties, I still knelt every night beside my bed to pray before I lay down beside my husband. With my narrow view of blessing, I knew there would be a miracle. Michael would wake up; the nightmare would be over. But it was to no avail.

As two weeks of rain lifted, my son's soul lifted also and flew home. Though I forgave everyone involved in this tragedy, there was one I didn't forgive—Mother Church, and by extension, Mother Mary. I continued to go to Mass for the sake of my children and husband, who needed some continuity in their lives, though I always cried during the music. Eventually I gave that up too. I was like a child whose mother has abandoned her, though I cloaked it in intellectual posturing about the church and religion in general.

It wasn't until the year 2005 that I came to terms with this long separation from my spiritual mother and was able to write that prayer. As usual, Lance was the catalyst for me to recover and repair my body memory. Every morning, we read a short paragraph given to us through the wonderful Peg Rubin from Jean Houston's Mystery School. This particular morning, we studied the German version of Parsifal and the Grail. In the story, Parsifal was stopped by a Holy Knight asking him why he was in battle gear on the holiest day in Christendom—Good Friday. Ultimately, he asked Parsifal when he had started to be angry at God. The question for the day, for the participants in Mystery School was: *When did you get angry and blame God, and what would have happened if a wise person had been there to give you support at that time?*

As Lance and I attempted to answer that question, I said that I had *not* blamed God, even when Michael died. And then, the tears came. I had an instant memory, a memory that said I had expected rescue and, yes, I *had* blamed God—and Mary.

I am in the Intensive Care Unit at Tampa General Hospital, at the head of the bed where Michael lays, unconscious. It has been days—I've lost all track of time. In the ICU it is always high noon. The smell is in my hair and skin; the smell of alcohol, chilled air, and sickness. My husband stands at the foot of the bed. We've been asked to wait for the doctor, an unusual thing. We wait anxiously for the few minutes a day we are allowed to be in this unit with our son, and now we have been allowed to stay past visiting time, past the mandatory twenty minutes.

Every day, I leave the hospital and go home, amazed that the world is still operating and people are still honking impatiently or turning up the music in their cars. I go home, numb and stoic, talk to my other children, thank those who are there to help, have oatmeal—the only food I can hold—and fall into bed where I mimic my son's coma.

Every day in the hospital chapel, I kneel and pray to the Blessed Mother. I await the miracle.

This day is different. The doctor finally comes in. He tells us there is no more they can do. Michael will be moved to a private room where we can be with him until the end. I receive this news in my numbness; the end of what? What is he talking about? And then, I see my husband's face. It records, in a way words cannot, what is being said. I lose all control and fall to my knees on the tile floor, the sound of the respirator drowned by a cry from me directly to God and Mary. I swear I will do anything they ask if they will spare my son. I cry out my grief, my pain, my anguish, my hands grasping the sheet on the bed, my head on the same level as Michael's.

No one touches me. No one comes near me. No one holds me. I am alone in the world, and I know the worst pain of all is upon me, and nothing will ever be the same, and I cannot die of it. And God, and Mary, do not hear me.

As I cried this morning in 2005, over thirty years later, the memory fell upon me with a full complement of senses: smell, taste, touch, and pain. Lance said that, if I was willing, it was time to work on this. As he talked about how we store emotions in the body, something we have worked on together, I realized why I had experienced such huge pain many years later when I fell to my knees when told my ex-husband was getting married. Pain was to be expected, but falling to my knees triggered not only that moment in time, but brought back the pain of the other time I had been struck down. I will share with you the process Lance took me through to find the core of this pain and transform it.

After a few moments of deep breathing and relaxation, Lance asked me to go, in my memory, to the hospital room on that day. When I was there, he asked me where I felt the emotion and what it felt like. I told him it was mostly in my heart, and felt like despair. Also, in the rest of my body, I felt tight. He told me to allow the emotions, breathe deeply into them, and then bring my ex-husband into the picture. I did this, and breathed deeply. "Now, tell him what you needed," Lance guided.

I had two voices in my head: one was telling my husband that I needed to be assured that we were not dying as Michael was dying. The other chided me by telling me how much he, also, was suffering, how he didn't want to know what I needed. He was in his own hell.

Lance asked me to silence that other voice and be strong in my need to be heard. I felt the tightness in my chest and body ease, and I anchored that feeling.

He then asked me to describe the emotion of feeling unsupported, carrying the burden alone. I felt that in the tightness in my shoulders, down through my hips.

He directed me to call upon my higher self for support to remove the burden from my shoulders.

I saw Jesus and Mary, then Kwan Yin, but then, rightly, Michael came and I heard the music I love so much: "You lift me up on angels' wings..." Michael the Archangel appeared and my Michael stepped into him and they lifted the burden from my shoulders, pulled the pain out through my skin. A glorious wave of peace went through my body.

Lance and I worked with this peace for some time, and today I can write about this event without feeling the heart-breaking grief. My heart swells with gratitude for the support I feel from the other side.

Through a gentler heart, I recognize this journey was necessary in order for me to understand my own relationship with God. The feminine and masculine parts of the Creator were not part of religious teaching, at least in the church of my childhood. I threw the most comforting part of God out with the church and embarked on a thirty-year quest for the goddess within and without. After the work on my anger toward God, Mary returned to me as part of the conversation I was having with my higher self and the representatives of my soul. No one was more surprised than I was. It was the middle of the night when I awoke to a female presence in my room and a voice of so much sweetness, my thorny heart bloomed into roses.

Mary Speaks

The only healing is love.
The feminine is love.
Go, spread love. Nothing else matters.
Give love to the children, the elderly.
Love those in war.
Tell them our hearts are meant for love.
We are hurting.
Love one another. This will heal your hearts.
Love my creation. Live in beauty.

Walk in love.
Through the application and intercession of love,
all things are possible.
I never left you. You are ready.

This gift of words from my other mother, Mary, came as I was wondering if it could be as simple as I was being told. Just love? What about those who didn't want your love? The answer came that it didn't matter. I was to be true, give of myself, and those who were ready would feel and hear the message. Those who were not were not my burden to bear.

Like some other poems I've written, the following arrived after a retreat, alone, filled with prayer and meditation. It is in the return to the "real" world that the difficulties arise. It's the same for those who attend workshops. How easy it all seems in the company of like-minded people!

After the Retreat

Bring home all that light,
pour it on the daisies,
lift the heads of pansies
toward heaven. Mystics
are multi-dimensional
knowers of all there is
to know. Feel sadness
in their ecstasy.
We are the blessed
gardeners of spirit,
misting the gifts of mystics
onto the seeds of family
and friends; growing love
between rows of men and

women. Drought ravaged
our lands for too long. We
inhale attar of roses,
bleed slowly from our
thorns; yet no matter
the depth of our wounding,
we find water. It flows,
warm and healing as
Magdalene's tears falling
on the feet of the Christ.

A Bell Awakened

The day's blow
Rang out, metallic—or it was I, a bell awakened...

This poem bears repeating. As Denise Levertov's words imply, one day we are "struck," and from that moment on, our whole self says and sings what it knows. It cannot be otherwise. That *certain day* is actually the result of an accumulation of minutes, hours, days, weeks, and years, gathered by us in an unaware gleaning of our fields of awareness. The Promise is that we will, if we maintain our focus on Truth and Love, reach that moment of awareness where our purpose and promises stand revealed, drenched in the light of knowing.

It is essential to know that each person's purpose, and thus their Promise on entering this world, is as individual as fingerprints. You are not like anyone else. Your path will not be my path. This work is simply to show you the steps I took to arrive in the garden of knowing that revealed my Truth. Without the guidance of those who went before me, my path would not have led me here in this lifetime.

My understanding of the imbalance on earth—demonstrated by war, the accumulation of material goods at the cost of spiritual knowing, anger, bodily mutilation (including the glorification of anorexia), and the abuse of children and women—demanded that I speak of the denial of the Sacred Feminine. I had been given the Knowing that was promised to me, I had followed the Truth to my heart's center, and now it was time to fulfill the Promise I had made before I came on this planet. I promised to honor the Feminine values represented by our Mother Earth, the Feminine Face of God, and all Her messengers.

Having found the Truth of my Promise, I made a solemn pledge in front of my altar, witnessed by those who have guided me here. I will honor the women and men of past cultures of cooperation who recognized the feminine and masculine principles as equally beneficial to earth's children. I will honor the pain and sacrifice of women who were born into times that relegated the feminine to the work of the devil. I will teach women, young and old, to release cellular memory of being "less than." I will teach women, young and old, to go back in time and honor their ancestors for their wisdom and sacrifice. I will teach women, young and old, to forgive those who stay unaware, but to honor themselves by not forgetting the cost of self-denial. I will teach women, young and old, to balance the benefits of their masculine side with the glorious light of their feminine selves. I will teach women, young and old, the dangers of "becoming men" to succeed in the workplace.

I will also share my heart's truth with them about women who have shut down their feminine knowing and put on a masculine aggression that causes great harm when it is in a place of power. Women such as Anne Coulter are wounded and have allowed their masculine to grow, as if on steroids, to protect their feminine side. Such women need our compassion; their anger does not come from health. And if, in the process, those wonderful men who honor the feminine find themselves in the stream of our gratitude, I will acknowledge them also. An equal balance within each man and woman of the feminine and masculine would result in heaven on earth.

The revelation that the feminine quest for the Grail takes place internally, and the wound of the Fisher King is the denial of the feminine, opened a whole world of knowledge and inquiry to me. The years spent in study, meditation, reading, prayer, and family lead me to a major facet of the one Truth as I see it. We are all meant to fulfill our soul's purpose on this planet. Not doing so is the source of disease and anguish in the human family. We have been promised peace and love in the energy of the Universe/God when we have seen the light and fulfilled our

Promise. That is the Promise made to us. Our lives begin and end with that one, simple instruction. I will fulfill my Promise through telling my Truth to the best of my ability from this day forward. Each of us has a different Promise to fulfill. Our lives are meant for discovering it.

The path is not easy—giving love and guidance to our children instead of the latest toys and quick-fix foods is a time-consuming task. However, if our Promise was to become parents and raise children who will rain light on this beautiful planet, we have no choice. If we have Promised to bring abuse out of the darkness and into the light, we can't do this by being nice. We must show it in all its horrors. As the poet Theodore Roethke put it so beautifully: "In a dark time, the eye begins to see." And if our Promise is to join in showing the imbalance of our planet—the heavy tilt to aggressive masculine energies resulting in war, stripping of nature, sucking up resources with no regard for future generations—then we must speak. The political and the spiritual are never separate.

When Mother Mary saw the life plan of her son, Jesus, she let him go. This was part of her Truth, her Promise, when she was born. When the Bible tells us God sacrificed his only Son for us, there is no mention of the agony of his mother. She bore him, raised him, and equipped him to live in this world. We know that he created a practice that honored the feminine before it was changed into a religion by his followers, so we know he honored his mother. How did the Inquisition and the witch trials arise from a religion founded by the followers of such a teacher and such a mother? The Truth was hidden; the Promise was buried.

It is part of my assignment to unbury it. It will require many of us and much guidance to accomplish our task before it is too late. There are those among us who think it is already too late, but I disagree. As I was shown, it is always the way of the Universe to move toward good and away from evil. Joining those who tell their Truth will create a body of love, diminishing the power of those who speak of fellow beings as "other" in order to give us an enemy to hate. Our lessons have been powerful. I offer an example. How many of us are afraid of snakes? As I write, the movies have again proven a point. The latest "horror" arrived last week in a movie about snakes loose on an airplane. I wonder if there are also terrorists on board. "Every fear wrapped up in one."

How did our fear of snakes come from our history as women? The snake is still wrapped around the caduceus, used by today's medical doctors. It was symbolic of women healers in ancient times, representing rebirth, regeneration, and healing. The goddess in many guises was wrapped in snakes, had the hair of snakes, and carried snakes—all for the purpose of projecting that all was as it should be in the world. Ancient ritual masks had the hair of snakes. Female faces surrounded by serpent-hair meant mystery and the wisdom of the Crone, appearing on ceremonial masks in many cultures. All of that was changed when Medusa (once the goddess Metis, meaning female wisdom) was changed into "mad Medusa," killer of children. What better way to turn the world against a woman than to tell us she killed her children?

In my cells, I had a horror of snakes. As a teenager, I fled on my bicycle in terror from a harmless Blue Racer. Was it from the ancient memory of women murdered for healing? I don't know the answer to that. What I do know is what happened to cure me of this fear.

Lance and I were in North Carolina, looking at property in hopes of having a spiritual center. We found a place I loved, a valley with a small house and a rushing stream sparkling over rocks beneath old oak trees. I sat on the bank, breathing in the fresh smell of swiftly moving water.

"There might be snakes here," I heard, and immediately left the bank and went to the car.

The next day, I had a massage in Banner Elk from a wonderful Reiki healer. She played a CD of Native American flute, and I fell into a semi-nap. I floated up above my body and saw myself sleeping on the bank of that stream. I watched with interest, not fear, as a huge python type of snake crawled out of the water and wound her slow and sinuous way up my leg. When she was completely out of the water, she laid her large head on my thigh and fell asleep with me.

When I awoke to find myself on Kelly's table amid the wonderful scents of ylang-ylang, geranium, and eucalyptus, I was amazed to find myself calm and peaceful. I felt like I had been visited by a wonderful being, and my fear of snakes has transformed into a healthy respect for things that might be dangerous to me in certain circumstances. I recognize the snake as a symbol of the spiritual for women and I apologize to Metis/Medusa for the lies told about her.

So, what is the next step? Once we have recognized the Truth of our own soul's direction; once we have recognized the Promise we received at our birth; once we have recognized the Promise we made before we arrived on this planet; what is next? Besides setting aside time each day for meditation, it is essential that we recognize the guidance that we have in our daily lives. It will save so much effort to know how to tune in. In the last section of this book, I will share the ways that I've learned to be in the flow of guidance and our heart/soul purpose.

As I write this section, opportunities for speaking out are arising every minute of the day. Usually, I don't watch television because it interferes with the other reception in my life—the direct contact with my guidance. However, I am traveling at the moment, teaching and attending to business, and have been given access to television as the Israeli/Palestinian horror heats up and the war between Israel and Lebanon begins. Stories of "our" soldiers in Iraq raping and murdering civilians are recited with fact-based precision; no faces, no family ties, and no funerals.

It is the same for the soldiers themselves, no matter how they return from war. In our practice and among friends and acquaintances, stories of acute depression and incidents of suicide are frequent enough to bear investigating, but we talk about the "brave" soldiers, not the wounded ones. As in no other war, many of these boys/men/women are National Guard weekend warriors who never expected to defend more than their downtown if a road rally got out of hand. The psychological implications of their participation, the children left at home while mothers go to war, are grossly underestimated.

Another story talked about Aryan Nation soldiers enlisting so they can learn from the experts how to make war. They slide through because so many are needed to conduct war and enlistments are down. And what happens to the Aryan soldiers? We know who their targets are, back at home, after that learning takes place.

For me, immunity to world news has been eroded by a year without television. It is as if the newsmen and women bombarding me with horrific photos from CNN and MSNBC are totally separated from the human suffering and emotionally attached to only one thing: their own political opinions. It is so obvious to someone who has returned to the land of photo ops from the intentional life of study and writing. I read that Diane Sawyer is lamenting the new technology that will show the "swelling" under her eyes. She is supposed to be our eyes on the world! Who cares about her puffiness?

There are, of course, exceptions, but the main Truth is that masculine energy on the planet is running amok and the innocent who are suffering in war have no place of sanctuary. They have become part of the news, their humanness obliterated by men, and women, with stone faces. No longer able to keep silent, I release myself to the promise I made—to say when the balance of energy in our world is corrupted and is leading us into a hell we cannot imagine. More of us must speak. Women in Afghanistan and Iraq, and those who live in war-torn countries all over this bruised planet, have spoken out and lost their lives.

All over the world, women are being silenced, whether by ridicule, the shrouding of their faces and bodies, or death. We must speak for them and with them. There is no longer any choice. Death of the spirit is the only possibility if good people keep silent. Silence in the service of good manners is resulting in death for those who need our voices. We must see the faces and fears of both sides and shine the light of love and sisterhood on them, before it is too late. "Bring home all that light and shine it on the daisies…"

This week, as I write, huge amounts of press have been lavished on Oprah and her best woman friend following the publication of an *O, The Oprah Magazine* article on friendship. In an amazing peek into the world of denial of the truth of women's friendships, the entire conversation centers on: "Are they or are they not gay." In everywhere but America, and possibly Canada, the wise man and woman know that the friendships of women provide a network of support, wisdom, and laughter. It is so ordinary as to lack notice. Girls go arm in arm in most countries, kiss each other affectionately on the street. Men interfere with this at their peril. It is preparation for a way of life that has disappeared in most industrial nations—the support system of the tribe. (See an article in Appendix I about the importance, the actual life-affirming qualities, of the friendships between girls and women.)

In my country, the artificially induced competition that descends upon girls in puberty destroys most of these friendships. The press is surprised to note that not *all* of them were caught in the roundup. They would be horrified to know that despite the advertising world's best efforts, we are coming together on the other side saying, "There you are! I missed you."

Several years ago, I attended a women's gathering in New York sponsored by Eve Ensler and Omega Institute. There were over a thousand women in this gathering and the energy was enough to power more than one space shuttle to Venus and back. Women from every walk of life and every ethnic background shared laughter and tears with women from Afghanistan, Iraq, China, and Africa. Mothers and daughters, including me and one of my daughters, shared stories with mothers and daughters from other continents. We found our commonalities to be so much greater than our differences that we had to look for the latter. Goods sold from South American women's cooperatives went to help the poor, and complimentary foot rubs were just for love. It was a joyous celebration of the best that women have to offer, shared in openhanded and heartfelt sisterhood. I will never forget it as long as I live. Perhaps that is what the pundits of cable are afraid of. We know where our power comes from—it is from within. We know where our power needs to be given—to those who are in need. It's too simple and also too deadly to the cause of competition.

How you choose to express your soul's purpose in your daily life and in affecting the world around us is known only to you. No one can tell you the best path, or how you will walk that path. I have shared with you my route. I ask that you read the last section where I will share with you the processes I use when learning and teaching. I pray they will be helpful to you. There is support in numbers. Women who come to my workshops are choosing to remain in contact and meet in a regular manner to encourage the work and take the arm of those who falter on the path. We are not alone when we follow our heart/soul purpose and promise and tell our truth.

Our strength is a bell sounding, leading others to play the music of their souls until a huge orchestra of vibration announces that love and peace have returned to the planet. Do not be surprised if the darkness and absence of melody seem to increase as we sing and play our Truth. There will be a fear-based reaction to this process that has already begun, but we have been promised that good will overcome evil, light will penetrate the darkness, and love will conquer all. That's enough encouragement to begin.

In my workshops, a process called "The Meadow" involves playing extremely evocative music and visualizing our female ancestors joining us, one by one, from the past into the present in a huge, flower-filled meadow. The visualization moves to the future, where we envision all our female descendants turning to face us, and then gracefully walking back in time to join us in the meadow and thank us for our efforts in the name of future generations. See Part Four of this book for the visualization.

The continuity of our line is a great comfort. It means that our work will benefit those who come after; not just benefit, but tell them that we were here and that we cared deeply. It is profoundly powerful to see the numbers of us, to see love and support all around us, and to join together for peace and the return of the Sacred Feminine to our world. Be filled with joy as the great-hearted of the world—women and men— tip our beautiful Mother Earth back into her rightful alignment so that our children and their children and their children will honor us for our Truth. We Promise them that we will be the Beings we were meant to be on this planet so that they may do the same. In this way, we return peace, love, justice, and beauty to their rightful place—the center of our lives.

Dialogue XVIX

I ask you to tell me if the book is finished. I know I have promised to write a last section of processes, but I need to know if the rest is complete.

My child, you have worked hard to bring this work to completion. The headache you are suffering means it is time to stop, for now. We will bring you more as time goes on, so don't say that the work is complete, only that it is finished, for now. Go ahead in a day or so and write the last section. When you have rested, we will tell you what else we want you to say. It will not be much. We are proud of you, and your task now is direct. You must speak when you are finished writing. That will be harder for you, but we will be here to encourage your efforts.

I want to speak, but always need help in speaking in an acceptable way, a way that won't create more friction instead of solutions.

You will know when you are guided from the heart, not the ego. You learned this already. Your speaking out will be done in groups and in your small family settings. Be prepared to not always be accepted for what you have to say. It still needs to be said. We will protect you and refresh you when your energy flags, as it is doing now. Rest. We will come back to you when the time is right.

I love feeling your support around me. I never feel alone. I will try to teach others to hear their guidance and feel this contentment.

That is part of your Promise. Until then, teach what you know. There will be those who will listen. The time is right.

Part Four:

WALKING YOUR PATH OF TRUTH

*The unconscious wants truth. It ceases to
speak to those who want something
else more than truth.*

—Adrienne Rich, poet

Each of us brings something alive in the world that no one else can.

—John O'Donohue, *Eternal Echoes*

Walking Your Path of Truth

You are ready to see your Promise and speak your Truth. You may already know, or at least have some idea, what this is. Even if you have full knowledge of your Promises (the one you made, the one made to you) and you are learning to speak your truth, the following work will support you. We who have buried the truth, and our desire for it, must reawaken the unconscious to speak truth, not old tapes, once again. There are many methods to do this, particularly therapeutic methods, but the amazing simplicity of some of the following exercises will open the pathway between you and your knowing through your own wisdom.

At or before birth, we received the skills, the receptors, and the knowing to uncover our personal purpose. The quest we embarked upon early in life may have presented a truly circuitous route to our souls' messages. The important thing is that we got here.

The energy that surrounds us, emanates from us, and fills the universe is one source. Science has shown us this through a microscope, though our greatest teachers have taught us this concept throughout time. Quantum physics and cellular biology came to the same conclusion: as Carl Sagan said so beautifully, we are star stuff. We are made of the same elements as our environment and our creator. Whatever we send out in the form of thought-energy resonates with the universe and returns to us what we have manifested. Being the universe, it follows the great dictum of non-judgment. If that is what you manifest, that is what the universe will send, without argument. When you feel joy in your being, you are sending out positive messages and receiving positive results. When your body feels in a state of confusion, indecision, sadness, lack, or any other negative emotion, you have been sending and receiving the wrong messages for your happiness.

Example: If you spend your morning prayer time cataloging your aches and pains and begging for help, you are telling the universe that you are attached to these aches and pains and desire more of the same. If you spend your early morning in gratitude for what is in your life that you love, you are attracting more of the same. And when you recognize this skill, you can attract other things into your life as well with a purposeful intention to do so. You can accept this on faith from your spiritual teachers or, if you are built that way, go to the science.

As always, I remind you that science is not my field, but people like Candace Pert, Bruce Lipton, and Deepak Chopra are excellent guides through the maze of cells and quantum guidance. I share with you, later in this section, an exercise with energy that I present in expanded form in my workshops and with personal clients. It's easy to do, requires no equipment, and you will never see your body/spirit connection and its abilities quite the same. It will assist you in finding your Truth and your Promises. You are not alone.

*Some women wait for something to change
and nothing does change,
so they change themselves.*
—Audre Lorde

We changed from being heart/soul oriented to being brain oriented. This is like saying that the emotions and purpose of my writing reside in the hard drive of my computer. To change ourselves, and then the world, we must return to the heart/soul energies. This is where wisdom resides. Trust the knowing of your heart. The heart's beat is in tune with the Universe. I've squandered untold energy in my life trying to become what makes others more comfortable. For many years, I worried about being too serious—of not being a "fun" person—and went to places and participated in things that were just not in my nature. We are all different, but we try so hard to fit someone else's idea of who they want us to be.

I remember vividly the last time I went to the golf club my husband enjoyed. I tried to be social, to walk up to strangers and say hello. This group of people was an important part of my mate's life. It should not be so difficult! I approached a trio of women having an animated discussion. When there was a pause, I introduced myself. They were warm and welcoming. This was easier than I'd thought! One asked me if I played golf. I said no, thinking of the hours away from my family and my writing that I was not willing to sacrifice. The second one asked if I played tennis. I said no, thinking of the organization involved in the club tennis scene and how getting my teenaged kids to their athletic events was all I could manage in between work and household duties and writing.

"My dear," said the third woman, a puzzled look on her lovely face, "What *do* you do?"

And before I could frame an answer, they had gone. I told my husband I just couldn't do this anymore—it was not my place to be. There was nothing wrong with the place; the club was absolutely gorgeous, the food was excellent, and the people were lovely. We just didn't have anything to share with one another at this point in our lives. I would relish sitting on their porches reading or writing. Oops—not the right answer. He felt I was being judgmental and not making the effort that would set all this right. I was not fun.

This played right into my doubts about myself, that I was "too serious" and needed to "lighten up." And, of course, there remained this age-old problem of needing solitude. Yet my friends and I enjoy each other's company, and I think my children and family do too. My mate tells me I *am* fun, and after years of persuasion, I began to believe him. I love going to concerts and feeling the music, going to dinner with friends or having them over while we cook. That's pure pleasure. This other thing was a more forced social expectation. Still, I felt unsure enough of my right to be who I was, as I was, to have struggled to change my way of being for years. It was time to quit trying. What would happen? Someone wouldn't like me. I would have to learn to live with that. And

I did. What I didn't know was that I was judging myself as harshly as I was being judged.

On Easter Monday of 2005, I received another visit, one I welcomed whole-heartedly. It was the last piece of the puzzle in the "Who am I?" question that has haunted me.

Dialogue XX

I awake with two lines in my head: Love in the heart is Heaven divine; this fountain of blessing is yours and mine.

I feel you there this morning. I'm glad. I've felt loneliness in your absence.

Good morning again, Beloved. What is it you wish to ask me?

Sometimes it seems difficult, even when all is well. I have this sadness deep inside. It permeates all of me to a lesser degree. When I read that laughter is a holy thing and I shouldn't take myself so seriously, I become sadder. I don't know how to be "light." I believe I have always been this way—I see pictures of me as a baby and a child and I look so serious!

Oh, my child. You must love you as you are. To force a nature upon yourself that is not yours is a terrible thing. Sometimes you see a baby and say, "What a solemn child! It's as if she carries the woes of the world." Sometimes this is true. Empathy and awareness can cause an underlying layer of sadness even when the top layer of humanness is content and happy.

When Lance asks me if I'm happy, he is concerned, not asking me to put on a mask. I am relaxed and contented, but I'm not verbally conveying happiness.

You need to accept yourself, dear one. You are as you are. You feel deeply. And yet you express this quietly and sometimes non-verbally. That is who you are. Pretending to have an expansive jolly nature will gain you nothing but heartache. Lightening the heart is another thing. When you need to do that, being with children will help you. All we have shared with you is in preparation for the Great Work.

What is the "Great Work"?

The universe is always moving. The Great Work is to keep it moving in the right direction—the direction of good. Many forces are at work on Earth that stall the energy from evolving into good. Selfishness and greed are mankind's negative tool for learning this Truth. The more you see your planet divided into the haves and have-nots, the more you will see how out of balance you are.

Are we too late to change it?

It is what it is. Many who try to right the balance in a peaceful way are demonstrating the power of good. But there is so much noise, so much jagged energy, it is hard for others to see their value. Only when the forces of good combine to be seen will change occur.

Once again I learn that love needs to be self-directed also, and understanding of the personality is best done at the level of energy. And that is what we will be practicing. Only by a huge change in the understanding of our personal energy and its connection to the energy of the planet will we create a world worthy of being passed on to our grandchildren. Being aware of energy is an early step in the process. Here, as I promised earlier, is an example you can use.

Beginning Energy Work

Have you ever walked into a room and approached a person only to feel repelled and actually back up a step? Science has proven that our heart energy field extends twelve to eighteen inches beyond our bodies and is measurable. As Stephen Harrod Buhner tells us, "The heart can act as a 'mind' or an organ of perception because approximately 60 percent of heart cells are neural cells, which function similarly to those in the brain." (If you are interested in the science, check out the work of the HeartMath Institute and the Harvard studies on the body as a non-linear system.)

The important thing here is that this is something we already *know* through our body/soul wisdom. Women in particular have instinctively reached out, literally, to the ill and the distressed to provide comfort, a process now recognized in the healing community as *Therapeutic Touch.* As twenty-first-century people, we are just more comfortable knowing that science has finally caught up to us.

Our body energy field extends several feet beyond our bodies. As soon as our field joins that of another person, it is as if our energies *feel* each other, forming an impression. Sometimes that impression creates the urge to back up; other times we want to step forward into what we know will be a wonderful hug. This knowing of the heart and body is natural emotional intelligence, a gift given to each of us at birth. It only asks that we reawaken to it. Our higher-self energy is infinite and connects to the universe. For practice at using your heart energy, try this exercise. Though I use it in a group, you can practice it with a friend.

132

Note: It is only because my work is primarily with women that the titles in these exercises are feminine. For those who have gotten used to the all-inclusive male pronouns over the years, it will take time to stop noticing the use of the feminine. (It is always true that these exercises are also useful for men.)

Heart Energy Exercise

Talk to your friend about doing this exercise. Pick a time where you will have at least fifteen minutes of quiet without interruption. Based on knowing that the heart energy extends twelve to eighteen inches beyond your body, approach your friend. When you are within that limit, close your eyes and focus on the energy between your heart and hers. Now, consciously create loving energy in your own heart and send it out to your partner. Ask her to do the same for you and feel the loving energy circulate between you. After a minute or two, open your eyes.

Back up and raise your arms straight in front of you until your hands are about twelve inches from your partner's hands. Now, raise your palms until they are facing the palms of your partner. Move forward slowly, bringing your palms closer to your partner's, until you begin to feel the energy radiating from her hands. When it is palpable, close your eyes and feel the energy pulsating between you. Hold for a moment.

Open your eyes. Back away a little and both partners open your arms between twelve and twenty-four inches, as if you're carrying a bunch of clothes from the line. Close your eyes again. Imagine and feel this space as an egg shape between you and fill it with energy. (If you need to bring the arms closer together, do so.) Cup your palms around that egg and feel it vibrate between you. Now, send the vibration of that energy into your partner in any place that you instinctively feel she needs healing. Have your partner do the same for you. Continue to hold that space until you feel the energy dissipate.

Talk with your partner about what both of you felt. This is a perfect example of how much we hold that we are unaware of. Some people will go into a room and say, "That person gives off bad vibes." This automatic reaction and the modern language are clues to our body energy power, but we don't "hear" ourselves. When and why we gave away our power and stopped listening to our inner soul wisdom is another book, but it is enough to know we have done it. Collectively, it is a modern loss. For you, as a human being, you can find where you gave away your power and recover it in a process I call *Sacred Feminine Visioning*. I will guide you through that process later in this section.

A great deal of information follows in the form of actual practices you can do to guide you along your personal path of discovery, leading to or enhancing your Promise and your Truth. Take your time with these. I lay them out for you in a particular order. Begin at the beginning, but if you find you are already familiar with one, or already practicing that process, move on as you see fit. Your intuition is the best guide for your study. Please commit to one practice several times and feel that it has become part of your being before you move to another.

These are very powerful, though very simple, tools. Each one will open you to a different knowing that you already possess. I encourage you to use and share any process that I have put in this book. It is only through the releasing of ownership of the Truth that we acknowledge the validity of everyone's Truth. I only ask that you use them in love and care, and only with those who are fully cognizant of why they are participating.

In the esoteric Judaism of the Cabalah, the Deep Self is named The Neshamah, from the root of Shmhm,
'to hear or listen': the Neshamah is She Who Listens,
the soul who inspires or guides us.

—Starhawk

Here we begin some processes and practices on how to enter or continue on the path of spiritual growth and uncovering or strengthening the Truth and Promise in your own life. Be *She Who Listens*: receive your soul's own guidance and you cannot fail. All of life is about this process. We would not have been set upon this path without support and wisdom. Soon, you will no longer need the guidance I'm providing here. My presence is only for you to draw upon as long as you welcome support in turning to your own spiritual wisdom. One day you will be creating your own processes.

Some choose to use these instructions once they learn them because they work and have become comfortable. Do whatever feels right to you. Inside each of us is the capacity to find our own ways of knowing and going. Trusting in your own inner wisdom is the end result that I pray for as I share with you my own personal path.

There were so many times when I needed the companionship of someone who had been *there* before me. When I reached the point where I trusted in myself and my intuition, I knew I would share that with others who resisted taking the twenty or more years I did to recover my own Truth. The following poem speaks to the process I underwent in my passage to sacred writing. It does not have to be this hard.

Sacred Poetry

Something larger than my self escapes
from me, paints portraits of spinning,
wheeling halo-surrounded stars
and names them. Returning from heaven,
I touch the colors and ask how I, who
cannot draw words, saw God and remembered.
I request the key to the lockbox of image, receive
only silence. The ecstasy of the right word, the
sublime colors of unity pour like mead hoarded
by jealous muses. I am the grapes of truth
growing on the gates of heaven. I lay drunk
with the expectation of the poet and mystic.

In the next section, I begin with a few simple necessities for living the soul-directed life and uncovering the power in your personal energy connections. Each of the journeys, meditations, or directives leads to the processes that follow and will heighten the learning of the others. Later, these practices can be selected in any order, based on what area is chosen by your heart's knowing. Some of you will find this information basic and will move on to other areas.

Another essential part of the journey is a journal. I hope you already have a journal for your sacred journey. If not, please begin one as you enter this process and journal each experience as you finish it. Put all of your thoughts, unedited, into your journal. This will be invaluable to you as you notice where you are, journey to your past, and ponder the truth of your future. Where you are going you cannot even imagine. The Truth is, the ability is in everyone. Not just St. John of the Cross or St. Teresa or Rumi. We can each access the place where the memory of our own wisdom lies and leave the authority figures behind.

Remember that the spiritual life is the *everyday life*. These practices are meant to help you honor the soul and spirit parts of yourself while you reflect them in your daily living. You are not being asked to become anything other than that which you are meant and desire to be. You will not become a recluse, a priestess in a temple in Egypt, or retire to the Himalayas to meditate—unless that is your soul's calling and your desire, of course. I am honored to be one of your guides into the most exciting time of your life, no matter what your age or circumstances. You have given me the gift of your attention in a world where you are bombarded with other energies. I do not take that lightly. I accompany you on this journey with my blessings and love, and I welcome any thoughts you would like to share with me.

Journeys and Practices

She was the single artificer of the world
In which she sang. And when she sang, the sea,
Whatever self it had, became the self
That was her song, for she was the maker.

—Wallace Stevens, "The Idea of Order at Key West"

We are the makers of our own world, the cocreators of that which was meant to be *me*. The most powerful tools for this work come from our own inside wisdom, our own singing. Our song is as individual as the calls of the birds, and as we open to our talent, the energy we flow on will bring us wonder, joy, and sweet surprise. Let's begin.

Note: My CD "The Promise: Walking Your Path of Truth" will lead you through the majority of the following exercises. I tell you in each case how much time you need to do the exercise. In a perfect world, you will add at least ten minutes to that time to journal and meditate about your experience. If you are not using my CD, you will need to record the visualizations/meditations in your own voice so you can receive the guidance with your eyes closed. It is more difficult to follow a meditation with open eyes. Even when the visualization is on my CD, I have written it in the book so you can use whatever music you want.

138

If an exercise is not on the CD, or you have not purchased the CD, choose instrumental music you love that is quiet and meditative. I also recommend several special CDs in Appendix II. I encourage you to use the same music every time you do a particular journey, since the music becomes an *anchor* that helps to lead you into the experience.

In all the following work, you need to be aware of the way/ways in which you communicate and receive information. It is fairly easy to figure out, and you probably already know. Wallace Stevens talks about the singer: a woman who is verbal enough to sing her world into existence. A later quote speaks of dancing from ear to ear—obviously a kinesthetic, or in the body, person.

To be sure about how you receive information and give information in the world, read the following guidelines for your answer. We all operate in three modes, primarily: visual, auditory, and kinesthetic. Still, we tend to use one more than the others—it is a sort of filter. Knowing which we are helps us to learn, so if you don't know, check yourself out in the following categories.

- *Visual*: (This is the mode for about two thirds of Americans.) Do you respond with the following?
  o "I just don't *see* that."
  o "Oh! I *see* what you mean."
  o "I wish you'd *clear* that up for me."
  o "I'll *show* you what I mean."
  o "Now, *picture* this!"

- *Auditory*: (This is the mode for about one sixth of Americans.) Do you *hear* yourself answering with the following?
  o "That *sounds* just about right."
  o "I try, but she just doesn't *hear* me."
  o "She tried to *tell* me, but her voice just *grated*!"
  o "*Listen* to this!"

- *Kinesthetic*: (This mode is also about one sixth of Americans.) Do you *feel* responses?
  o "I have a *feeling* about that."
  o "I just don't get a good *feel* from his information."

o "That really *touched* me."
o "I'm a *hands-on* kind of person."

As you begin to do exercises to get in touch with your inner wisdom and higher knowing, it will really help to be aware of your learning style. Then you can *listen* to the voice, *feel* the energy, or *see* the scene. For us to hear, feel, or see the energy and guidance we are receiving, quiet is important. Since I'm visual and auditory, I frequently use those types of words in my directions, though I make an effort to include all the senses. Feel free to substitute words that are closer to your experience. For instance, when you are led into an environment—like a garden—a visual person will see the colors of the flowers, an auditory person will add waterfalls and birds, and a kinesthetic person will touch the flowers and feel the breeze or the texture of the seats. There are many things you can do to enhance the experiences that follow.

Essentials for Beginning
Creating Sacred Space

Do you have an altar at home? A personal space where you can be alone and quiet for a few moments in the morning or evening, or for extended study and meditation? If not, it's time to create one.

Suggestions

Many have chosen their bedroom as the only possibility for a small, sacred space. It can be a simple end table on which you place a cloth (I use a silk shawl), or an antique table built to be an altar. That you have a designated space for soul work is what matters. On that table you will place several items that are special and evocative to you. The list runs from statues to feathers to small stones to family pictures. Water and flowers bring nature into your space. A candle (or candles) is an excellent addition, along with sage or a scented stick that can be burned to purify your space. Remember to satisfy your personal tastes: candles for smell and light; music for the ear; feathers, stones, fabric for touch; sage or incense for smell. They are important, since there must always be an intention to create sacred space for you and you alone. This is your space, to be entered by invitation only. Teaching others respect for your space will encourage them to expect respect of their own space.

My personal altar is draped with a lovely silk scarf from Tienda Ho and holds a statue of a seated Kwan Yin, the Goddess of Compassion (a gift from Lance). An alabaster statue of a woman holding a child anchors the other end. Candles, a small purple dish with sage, a malachite heart, and a sprig of lavender are some of the other things I love. On the wall above the altar is a framed photograph of a pregnant woman, a reclining, sensuous Rubenesque woman, and an Alaskan sea-spirit ink drawing—a gift from my sisters. A tapestry of the Tree of Life completes the space.

Below, on a shelf, are items I use when I pray or meditate at my altar: books, cards, matches, a small stereo, CDs, extra candles, and sage. I hope you can sense the theme of the feminine in my altar.

Additional sacred space created for a couple, a family, or an organization is also recommended for a complete and intentional spiritual life. Lance and I have created a second altar in our work space with items from both of us, and he has a personal altar with his own items for his private prayer and ritual.

Our home altar, in the living room, contains items that are important to both Lance and me and the work we do in the space: heart-shaped stones, a double candle shaped like a man and woman, sage, flowers, found items such as bird feathers, and items we have created specifically for the space. Above our altar is a heartbreakingly beautiful painting of Isis and Osiris by Susan Seddon Boulet, a tribute to the love and sacrifice required in being a couple. Below, on a shelf, resides a crystal singing bowl with which we begin workshops, plus cards and books for inspiration, extra sage, and matches.

We begin our day, whenever possible, at the altar. When we have an important day ahead or decisions to make, we create a ritual at the altar to invoke our highest good and the best result possible. When we teach a workshop, we begin with a ritual at the altar to create sacred space for the group.

Try to have a source for music in your room, though this is not necessary for everyone. Some people are more auditory than visual, so music is very evocative for them. Promise yourself that you will come here once a day, at least, to envelope yourself in a place that is not of the world.

Suggested Ritual

If you like sage, it's nice to begin your meditation or exercise by lighting pure, hand-harvested white sage and then blowing out the flame. (Native American wild-gathered is best. It can be found in stores that carry items for ritual.) Guide the smoke over your altar and around yourself, purifying both for your purpose. Others choose to use incense sticks for this purpose. Look into the source of these items and choose what feels clean, clear, and intentional for your altar. Lance and I never teach a workshop without purifying the space, whether it's in a hotel or a church.

Some don't like scents or smoke in their space. They choose to visualize clear light washing over their altar and through their bodies, cleansing them of the accumulation of stress and other people's energies. This is particularly useful for those who are envisioning healing.

After purifying your space, add any additional items or rituals, such as lighting the candles, praying, or invoking your guides and/or angels. You will feel guided as soon as you dedicate your altar to this purpose. For me, music is right in certain instances, guided visualizations can be helpful for healing, but silence is often the thing I need most.

Other Additions

Try adding different activities or items to enhance your daily meditation/prayer. I find cards useful because they are a *visual* manifestation of your intentions for that particular day. For instance, after calling on your guides or angels for information, you can shuffle and spread a deck of cards—angel cards, healing cards, etc.—and follow your intuition on which card to choose to enhance the information you are getting.

I sometimes use my Archangel Cards (see Appendix II) after asking for guidance in a particularly difficult situation. I will shuffle them as long as I feel I need to, then sometimes my guidance will tell me to cut them and choose a card, or I will spread them in a curved shape and choose one. Sometimes I hear the guidance to imagine the head and feet of this shape and see it as a human body. Then I will choose a card from the part of the body that is suggested by my request for guidance. For example, the heart for relationship, the throat for communication, or a part of the body that needs healing for information on how to go about that process.

About a year ago, I had cause to ask for support in a choice I was making—an everyday choice, but an important one. If it was true that I chose, unknowingly, illness in order to rest, it was time to make another choice. My son and a friend were coming to attend a music convention, one that Lance had encouraged and done much research for. It was generous of him to prepare the way in Los Angeles for these young men. He invited me to go, stay in the hotel while they networked, and go to dinner and music with them in the evening. I knew that the best thing for me would be to stay home, even without a car, because I would accomplish so much on my book. Without a car would be a bonus!

The voice of my conscience said that it was the least I could do to go, since Lance had done so much to help *my* son. Another voice, the voice of my guidance, said I should check in with my altar and my angels. I read the daily guide from my Jean Houston program, and it was about using my gifts in fertile ground. I put oils in the burner on my altar—mint and orange—and held the angel cards to my heart, asking how I was to best serve my gifts and also honor my mate. I shuffled the cards and drew the top one.

It was a card featuring Archangel Metatron, and was titled **Prioritize!** *Focus on your highest priorities. I will help you. What's your calling? What makes your heart sing? When you focus on these areas, your joyful energy increases, which benefits everyone. Take charge of your schedule and spend more time on projects and activities close to your heart. Make choices that honor and support your life's mission.*

As if that were not enough confirmation, I was drawn to another card midway into the deck. I turned it over and saw Archangel Ariel with a lion. Her card was **Courage**: *Be courageous and stand up for your beliefs. In this situation, you need to act upon your convictions, even if others disagree. As you stand up for your beliefs, you're a role model for others. This is an important form of spiritual teaching, in which your example gives others courage to also stand up for their own principles.*

I wrote in my journal that I didn't believe I had ever been more powerfully responded to by the angel cards. There was no doubt my direct question had been answered in a direct manner. When I told Lance my decision, he was supportive and urged me to follow my guidance. I know that I would have anyway, but what a gift to have that partnership!

Will I use Ariel's courage, the courage of the lion, to stand in my Truth?

The most important part is to *hear, see, sense,* or *feel* your guidance and then follow it immediately, without hesitating and questioning—as long as it feels pure and in your highest good to do so. The more you stay aware with your senses, and each one of you has a different sensing modality, the more natural it will become. Listen to suggestions of others you trust, but always know your own guidance system will alert you when these are useful or not useful.

Now that you have created a sacred space for your spiritual life, it is time to rediscover a sacred space that you carry with you—created by your own natural inner wisdom. Once you have this inner space clearly in your sense of yourself, you can access it anytime.

How to create and enter peaceful, sacred space anytime, anywhere

First, you must remember how to breathe. We have become a world of shallow breathers. This restricts our oxygen, keeps negative particles from leaving our cells, and makes us tired, restricting our sense of emotional resonance with our feelings. The first step to physical and spiritual help is to return to our natural way of breathing. Remember how a baby breathes? Or a puppy? You can see the rise and fall as they breathe with their whole bodies. Practice breathing deeply.

Inhale through your abdomen, watching it expand until it can't go any further. Exhale, feeling your belly cave toward your backbone, expelling all the air from your lungs.

Continue to practice this for about two minutes. Do this every day, several times a day. This will also take you into a moment of silence, since you can't do this and speak or listen to someone or something else when you are concentrating on your breathing. Silence is most important.

Also, if you do this type of breathing before making a decision or responding to a situation, it gives your intuition time to bring up a proper response. Proper breathing is the most important physical part of spiritual practice.

You will not always have access to the sacred space you created in your home or office when you are in a stressful or difficult situation, or when you simply want to spend a few moments there. Following your relaxing breathing, it is possible to have this space at your fingertips anytime, as I do with my Maui waterfall experience. When you *are* in your sacred space, in front of your altar, do the following practice, which includes *Somatic Intuitive Training.* This process will teach you to create "portable" sacred space that you will take with you wherever you go.

Practice

When you are in front of your altar, play a favorite quiet meditation piece or be in silence. Eyes closed, practicing just being, breathe deeply. Then ask yourself the following question.

"Can I relive or remember a pleasant time in my life that confirmed my spiritual knowing?"

These do not have to be blinding "aha!" events, but moments when literal time slowed or stood still and you were aware of the beauty and connection of the universe and/or yourself to something larger and more profound than daily life. You may also remember a powerful time when you awakened to a knowing about your purpose or commitment, or simply a peaceful feeling. One of my strongest emotional triggers, in addition to Maui, is the feeling of holding an infant in my arms. This can take me directly to bliss.

When you have a moment in mind—frequently the first one you'll think of is in nature—remember everything you can about that time and place. For instance, use all of your senses to see the scene, smell it, hear the sound of it, and if there is a taste or feel, bring that back to your mind and body also. Take your time.

You can come back to this place anytime you need to, simply, after learning the next process—Somatic Intuitive Training. Think of this as creating a portable sacred space! Just follow the simple guidance and practice it for at least a week, a few minutes during the day or before bed, and you will always have a way into peace.

Somatic Intuitive Training

This guidance comes from **Somatic Intuitive Training**™, a method taught and certified by Lance Ware, and is condensed from his lecture on "Living an Intentional Life." Instructions are also on one of his CDs, *Heart and Soul Meditations*, which are listed in Appendix II.

- *Find a safe, quiet place where you will be free of interruptions for at least twenty minutes.*
- *Play music, if possible, that calms you. (See music in Appendix II.)*
- *Close your eyes and breathe deeply, inhaling and exhaling from your belly/abdomen at least five times.*
- *Clear your mind as much as possible; go in your memory to a place where you feel peace. (As you practiced earlier.)*
- *Notice when your body feels relaxed. (Shoulders soften, chest releases, etc.)*
- *When you are as relaxed as you can be, press your thumb and index finger together and begin storing these peaceful relaxing feelings for use anytime, anyplace. Use all your powers of concentration and visualization. Hold your fingers together and count back from ten to one, breathing in and out slowly and deeply as you count.*
- *Breathe in and out deeply a few times.*
- *Now, with your eyes still closed, think of another time in your memory where you felt peaceful, calm, and happy. When you have*

147

this feeling, again, press your fingers together to store these feelings of peace and calm. As before, count back from ten to one, breathing in and out slowly as you count down.

- *Open your eyes, release your fingers, and get up from your place. Look up and around, get up, and walk for a minute and sit down again.*
- *Close your eyes and press your fingers together and experience the calm relaxing feelings you placed there. Stay in this position for a few moments, then open your eyes and release your fingers.*
- *You have now stored this feeling of your special place in your thumb and index finger. This process intentionally anchors a state of relaxation, as you use all of your concentration and visualization. Repeat this step morning and/or night for a week. Then, whenever you need to relax, breathe deeply, press your thumb and finger together, and you'll re-experience the calm and peace you've been practicing.**
- *Write how this practice works for you in your journal and compare these writings as you practice.*

* A note about the thumb and forefinger being the peaceful calming place: when you do this over and over, you are increasing the depth of the feeling with more samples of peace and serenity. When you go to these fingers, or anchors, the feelings of peace and calm will be more intense. If you were to receive training in S.I.T., you would learn how to use other locations for other feelings and learn how to stack and collapse these anchors. For our purposes, using the relaxation location is enough. (See www.IsisInstitute.com for more information on Somatic Intuitive Training.)

Being able to enter your peaceful place anytime, day or night, is a powerful gift from your physical self to your spiritual self. And the process is nearly invisible! If you are in a work setting and stressed, simply press your fingers together, feel your body and mind relax, and continue on with your day. If you can close your eyes, do so, but it's not absolutely necessary. In a meeting, simply have your hands lower than the table or desk and squeeze your fingers together. The feeling of relaxation will be instant. The wonderful thing is that you are the creator of this place. It is yours to summon at will. No one can tell you no.

This may seem too simple to you, but remember that your body is a finely tuned emotional, mental, and energetic instrument—the Universe did not make us so that it would be hard. Your body can do the work you ask of it, and its memory for what you have installed is hardwired. These two exercises, the deep breathing into a remembered scene and S.I.T., will make this scene, or others, a part of your being. You can call this memory up at any time.

What Makes Your Soul Sing (or Dance)?

Before you begin the other processes, I want you to answer this question in your journal. Remember the Wallace Stevens poem about singing your life. This voice or instrument comes directly from the higher self and the soul. If you have page one in your journal available, please write your answer to "What Makes My Soul Sing?" on page one. It is so important to listen to your inner knowing, and this is a question you must have an answer to. If you say you don't know, you have work to do to open to your own wisdom. I think you do know. Put this in essay form or numbers one through ten or any way that feels right to you. Theodore Roethke, a wonderful poet, said, "I hear my being dance from ear to ear." What makes your being dance from ear to ear? Before you begin, do the following:

Open your journal and have a pen ready. Go to your quiet space and breathe deeply, as you have learned. Follow this with a visualization of your special place and place your hands over your heart. Breathe deeply and ask yourself the question. **What makes my soul sing?** *Press your thumb and forefinger together and count to ten. Release your fingers and listen to your heart.*

I'll share with you what happened when I did this exercise, but write first, read later. Take all the time you need. When you are finished, read it aloud to yourself and then add anything that comes up as you read. You may want to meditate on this, or think about what came up and

150

what might have surprised you. Always keep this in mind when you are working on finding your Promise. What makes your soul sing is a clue to your work on the earth.

What Makes My Soul Sing?

1) I ask myself this question and my gaze turns toward the door. My love sits on the porch, face raised to the sky in pure knowing; he is where he makes sense. A sunflower, he sways with the breeze that sweeps the valley, putting out leaves in the shape of poems. He has come home.

2) Each hour an unearned gift on the way. The curled head of a bird-of-paradise rising from its stalk in flaming glory; the hawk banking against clouds, his mate a shadow dancer; a mere peek of pink hinting at the perfumed glory of a Peace rose soon to bloom. All of this before lunch, leaving the rest of the day for...

3) And what about me? The beauty and his love hold me here, tinges of sad separation from family and friends are washed around my edges with a fine blush—a different singing.

I, too, receive the unearned gifts of flower, bird and breeze. Not sacrifice but choice identifies my place, my mate, my work. Tonight, together, we will sit on the porch, faces raised like moonflowers to the stars, pine trees whispering the valley's secrets. It will take a long time to learn all they have to tell, but we are patient, rocking toward heaven.

Another day I will feel the presence of my children and grandchildren in my space, and know that the answers are many. And as I sit and write, I am in joy. My soul sings many different songs.

Finding Your Personal Guidance

Each one of us has a unique guidance system complete with energetic guides. These are signs along the path, aids to our travel. Some call these angels, some recognize the energy of loved ones who have died, and others are gifted with strangers who arrive in meditation or dreams. And remember your own innate wisdom, stored in your heart/soul and your higher self. It doesn't matter how you see or feel this guidance, as it will be what you ask for. It is essential that we always begin with prayer or meditation and a pure heart. Nothing that comes from that space can be other than your true self. The first and most important part of the process is to access your *higher* self, eliminating the possibility that you are simply downloading your ego's idea of guidance.

Accessing your higher self will also make all relationships in your world improve. The ego acts from fear, protecting its territory. It has a very strong instinct to protect you, and that's important, but you will know through your personal wisdom that it is just protecting territory, not the genuine you. For example, children in a sandbox or in the toy box:

"Those are mine!"

"No, they're mine!"

A fight ensues, tears, anger, and absolutely no joy in the sandbox or the toy box. We can extrapolate that to the deepest, most tragic conflicts going on in the world today—mine/yours, us/them. The cycle can be stopped when we all subjugate the ego to the higher self. There are several ways to access your higher self, and that space will, in turn, introduce you to your other guides when you want to learn more about them.

Accessing Your Higher Self
Part I

This visualization is track 1 on the CD *The Promise: Walking Your Path of Truth*
Time: 5 minutes, 41 seconds plus time to journal

Begin the CD or your own recording.

Sit quietly, close your eyes, and take several deep breaths, being totally aware of your abdomen expanding on the inhale, deflating toward your spine as you release your breath. Do this until you are aware that your breathing has slowed and your muscles are relaxing. (Relax your shoulders.) (Pause)

The purpose of this exercise is to become aware of your higher self and the feeling of its energy. That's all you will be asked to do.

Focus your awareness on the heart and the energy surrounding it. If you like to visualize color, the heart color is green. Raise that energy—see it visually or feel it physically—through your throat, up through your head, and watch/feel it flow out through the top of your head. Imagine you still have a soft spot there like a baby has and allow your heart energy to come from that spot like a fountain and fall softly around your whole body. Breathe deeply, inhaling the green heart energy into and through your whole body. Keep breathing deeply. (Pause)

When you feel completely at one with the energy—meaning that you are completely comfortable in your body/heart—you are going to see, feel, or sense your higher self energy. This energy is not attached to ego in any way, but to your highest purpose. Right now, there is a shimmer of energy above your head. This is where your higher self abides. The energy of your higher self is described as purple or silver, but it can also be white or clear. Trust your intuition. Breathe deeply as you sense the higher self energy gathered just above your head. This is the energy that connects you to all that you can be, and to your guidance. Breathe. (Pause)

Now let the energy flow down and into your body, simply to relax and calm you. Let the energy go all the way down into your feet and then all the way back up to your head. As you do, listen for or sense any information your body and/or higher self are giving you. Keep breathing. (Pause)

Now relax and let the energy absorb in your body. See the top of your head close, bringing you back to body energy. Take a few moments to enjoy this feeling, however it expresses in your body.

Open your eyes and return to the room when you are comfortable, then write about this in your journal.

Accessing Your Higher Self
Part II

This visualization is track 2 on the CD
Time: 7 minutes, 3 seconds plus time to journal

When you have practiced Part One several times, journaling what you were feeling and are completely comfortable, proceed to Part Two. You will notice that the first part of this exercise follows the process you have already practiced in **Accessing Your Higher Self: Part One**.

Relax, sit quietly, close your eyes, and take several deep breaths. Be completely aware of your abdomen expanding on the inhale, deflating toward your spine as you release your breath. Do this until you are aware that your breathing has slowed and your muscles have relaxed. (Relax your shoulders.) (Pause)

Become aware of your heart and the energy surrounding it. If you like to visualize color, the heart color is green. Raise that energy—see it visually or feel it physically—through your throat, up through your head, and watch, feel, or sense it flow out through the top of your head. Imagine you still have a soft spot there like a baby has and allow your heart energy to come from that spot like a fountain and fall softly around your whole body. Keep breathing deeply. (Pause)

Take the green energy into your body, washing you from head to toe. When you feel completely at one with the energy—meaning that you are comfortable in your body/heart—see or sense the shimmer of your higher self energy above your head. Just enjoy being aware of your higher self energy. Breathe—deeply and slowly. (Pause)

Now, see or sense the way your higher self is connected to your body and then, at its other end, blends into the air above your head. This is the part of your energy that connects you to your guidance. It is a conduit between you and the universal voices. Visualize or feel this connection. Breathe. (Pause)

Ask your higher self to speak to you in a way you can understand, a way that is outside of the ego and your thoughts. Sit quietly and breathe deeply— you will sense a communication. It will not necessarily be a voice that you hear. It may be an energetic vibration, a knowing, or a visual sense. Anything is possible, but you will know. Remember that this is your own knowing and intuition, freed of the pressure of the ego. Listen deeply for the wisdom of your higher self. (Pause)

When the voice or feeling comes, ask your higher self if it has anything to add to your question, "What makes my soul sing?" Your higher self is the first step into your guidance. Again, some will actually hear a voice, but that is not the norm. We can sense the higher self because we recognize its energy—it is part of us. (Pause)

Be attentive. Continue to breathe deeply. Your higher self is a safe place. It will not create feelings in your body that the ego creates. You will have a sense of peace and calm. A gentle counseling spirit is higher self wisdom. Listen quietly for as long as you feel you are hearing direction or simply receiving energy. (Pause)

It is time to thank your intuitive, wise self for anything that came to you in this exercise. (Pause)

Open your eyes, and write in your journal any information you received in this meditation, or any feelings you had about this meditation.

Don't wait. Our brains get busy and we are unable to recall exactly what occurred. Repeat this exercise daily until it feels natural and normal to have conversations with your higher self and your guidance.

When you are comfortable with what you have just completed, you will find yourself able to go to this place of the higher self when you want to. Say you are talking to someone and need to get out of the ego's space, or you feel reactions within yourself that are ego based and you desire to go to your higher wisdom; close your eyes and visualize your higher self energy. If a heated argument is starting with a loved one or you have conflict with a colleague or family member, go to your higher self and speak from there. It will change everything. You will soon find, with practice, that you will consciously enter your higher self before beginning a conversation that may be emotionally loaded. This is another tool in addition to the calm and peace stored in your fingers through S.I.T.

Now that you have learned to listen to your higher self, part of your own energy system, it's time to approach your outer guidance. The only difference is that in accessing your higher self, you are tapping into the wisdom and intuition of your own guidance, or energy, system.

Outside guidance—or that guidance which comes from angelic presences, guides, or any other part of the energetic system—is brought into us through connecting to other energetic beings. That is why it is so important that we tune in to our higher selves, our intuition, and our wisdom first. It is essential that we recognize those energies which are healthy for us and those which are not. Some people's energy simply drains us. There are names for these beings—energy vampires being one that is used in the business world. Some people walk into a room and plug into your power. It is their way of being. They are not evil, simply needy. You choose not to be available to this or any other energy without your permission.

Beginning the process in your sacred space is mandatory. Saying a prayer of protection to whomever or whatever you see as the good in the universe is also helpful. These prayers can be of your own making or those that have been provided by others.

Whenever Lance or I work with healers or health care providers, we remind them to put protection around themselves. It is so easy for empathetic, caring people to absorb the energies of those they are in contact with. It is even easier to protect yourself from other energies. For instance, Lance and I use this prayer whenever we get in the car to go somewhere or begin work. It is a prayer written by James Dillett Freeman, and accompanied two Apollo missions to the moon.

The Prayer for Protection

The light of God surrounds us;
The love of God enfolds us;
The power of God protects us;
The presence of God watches over us.
Wherever we are, God is, and all is well.

You could certainly rewrite this in any way that is personal to you, or create a whole new prayer for yourself. The intention is to allow into your space only that which is in your best and highest good. Prayer, light, focused intention, and the use of your sacred space are all part of this process. Each of us has guidance that is personal and particular to our lives, our ancestors, our spiritual beliefs and practices, and how we live. Holy, loving guidance is a gift from the universe that was once seen as normal and part of everyday life. You can return to this time simply by signaling your intention to your guidance that you are ready.

Once you have protected yourself through love and light, it is time to contact your guidance. Light your candle and then light, and blow out, the sage or incense. Waft the smoke from the sage over the altar, over yourself, and throughout the room, saying whatever words feel comfortable to you to set the mood. I simply say:

"I come here with an open heart and am ready to receive that which is in my highest and best good. I welcome any who wish to be with me in this holy work."

Bring in any other ritual that feels right to you in your sacred space. When I work with my guidance, for instance, I like to use the crystal singing bowls. They are tuned to a certain chakra in the body, and help in communication. There are as many ways of connecting as there are personalities in those who desire guidance. As you grow in this way, you will find or invent your own methods of spiritual preparation. May you have a fruitful journey.

Beginning Practice for Receiving Guidance

This visualization is track 3 on the CD
Time: 5 minutes, 20 seconds plus time to journal

Begin the CD or your own recording.

Sit comfortably, close your eyes, and breathe deeply and slowly from your abdomen, as you have practiced in the prior work. (Pause)

Open your heart to that which is only in your highest and best interest. Imagine light flowing into your heart from above. Go to your higher self, or simply stay in your heart if that feels right to you. Breathe. (Pause)

See or sense the light energy flowing into your body from far above—the choice of color is intuitive. Feel the openness. Remember that the light energy above your head is the place of your higher self and connects you to your guidance. In this case, you are asking for guidance from outside of yourself, so reach out with your energy. Simply have the intention that you will receive guidance and that it will be in your best and highest good. Be patient in your sacred space. Breathe.

In time, you might hear an actual voice; others enjoy a feeling of warmth and protection; others a buzzing energy; some feel an actual physical touch, always comforting and wise; and others just relax more deeply. Whatever comes to you in this space is right for you. There are no rules or right ways of being other than the absolute necessity to be present to your highest good. Stay in this comfortable position for as long as you desire, breathing deeply and slowly, being aware at all times of the love and peace in your heart's space, and holding your intention to receive loving guidance. Continue to breathe deeply. (Long Pause)

When you are ready, say a brief thank you to the Universe/God for your ability to pursue your sacred purpose in whatever way feels right to you, and open your eyes.

The more often you practice this same process, the easier it will become to contact your highest guidance when you need it. Always journal the results of your practice—as hard as it is to believe, you will not remember. Always extinguish candles or sage before you leave your sacred space. Leave it as you want it to be when you return.

As you create an altar or reinvigorate your current altar, your daily presence there will bring about change in the way you "hear" guidance. I have received notes, calls, and e-mails from many participants in my workshops, and I know they adapt the idea of guidance to their own way of being. For example, following their meditation/altar work, some are very comfortable with shuffling, pulling, and reading an angel guidance card, consulting The Runes or The Tarot, or opening a book at random to ask for guidance. Many books exist for this express purpose, but any book you are drawn to that is created for spiritual work will do. Many are able to ask for guidance before sleep and receive it in their dreams. Be sure you write any insights immediately upon awakening. A dream journal next to the bed is a wonderful thing to have.

In my workshops, I love using anthropologist Angeles Arrien's work. Her process of looking deeply into symbolism helps us see where we are now, where we are going, and our preferred ways of working to get there. Her interpretation of the Tarot Cards brought me to see their significance in our modern world in a new and symbolic way. Sometimes, the ancient teachings require a modern and gifted oracle. Once in a while, doing the *Preferential Shapes Test* she has developed is very useful. As an adjunct to meditation, we can do short versions of this exercise to see where we currently are on our spiritual path using her studies of symbols in the everyday. Our ways of receiving are many and wonderful, and those we receive from are also many and wonderful.

When you feel completely comfortable in your sacred space, and with the last exercise, *Beginning to Receive Guidance*, you are ready for the process of consciously asking for guidance from personal guides and knowing who they are in your daily life. Soon you won't have to ask. **Take all the time you need.** All will unfold in its own time, depending on your ability to relax and enter your personal sacred space. It's very important that you have a ritual that you repeat each time, just as you set a memory (also known as your anchor) in your thumb and finger earlier. That ritual—whether it's a particular prayer at your altar or in bed or a particular way of blessing your space—will set the tone for the requests you are about to make.

Sometimes, the process of visualization is instantly successful in identifying your guides. When you're ready to follow the visualization, be sure you have the required time set aside where you won't be interrupted. If you can, allow thirty minutes so you can write and meditate after the actual process. Play the guided CD or your own recording, but once you have become familiar with the process, see Appendix II for music recommendations or feel free to use your own favorite music that is quiet, peaceful, and long enough to continue to the end of the visualization. I find that, early on, it is an excellent anchor to use the same music. The music invokes the previous experience and builds on it.

Visualization
Greeting Your Personal Guides

This visualization is track 4 on the CD
Time: 14 minutes, 18 seconds plus time to journal

Begin the CD or your recording. Settle quietly in a safe place where you will not be disturbed.

Close your eyes. Breathe deeply. Inhale, deeply, into your abdomen, feeling it tighten, like a drum. Slowly exhale until you feel there is no more air in your lungs. Do this at least five times. (Pause)

Place your attention on your heart. Feel the energy surrounding your heart. See it as a color, if you'd like. Feel the comfort in your heart. You are soothed by this wonderful music and your beautiful heart. (Pause)

Now, imagine a garden. The garden itself is your creation—full of your favorite flowers, trees, water. The garden of your spirituality can be entered in any way you find natural—through a gate, an open door, down a path. You are the creator of this space, so see it exactly as you would like to see your garden—in the middle of a forest, a backyard, by a river. This is the garden that is in your heart's space. See or sense where you are as you are about to enter this beautiful garden in your heart. (Pause)

Step into your garden. Hear the sounds—if there are birds, what kind of birds? What do they sound like, look like? Hear, feel, or sense the breeze rustling the leaves. What kinds of trees and flowers are here, if you have created trees and flowers? Be aware of their colors, vibrantly and energetically alive. Breathe. (Pause)

Soft golden light is flowing down into the center of the garden. Take some time now; explore the beauty and intricacy of your creation. You have only two intentions here; to relax and greet at least one of your guides. The relaxation alone is a gift. Remember to breathe. (Long Pause)

In the center of the space, beneath the light that glows like late autumn sunshine, you'll see a place where two or more can sit comfortably. It could be large smooth boulders, cushioned chairs, or stone benches—anything you can imagine. Create this seating in your perfect image of comfort. Breathe. (Pause)

Go to that place and sit down, quietly, and feel the texture of the seat on your body. Is it rough, smooth? Sit with your hands resting in your lap. Enjoy the warmth of that light flowing down over you. Feel the soft air on your cheek and smell the air. Be completely in your garden. (Pause)

There is a slight motion nearby, moving the air. Someone has joined you, choosing another seat, beneath the light. Can you feel their energy? Can you see them behind your closed eyes? Can you hear them? Can you smell their individual scent? Breathe. (Long Pause)

When you have a feeling for who is there, ask them to tell you their name, if you don't already know. This may be a guide that is familiar to you. (Pause)

Feel the energy of this person. Nothing can exist in this garden that you do not want here. Only good can come into this place from your heart's desire. If you feel that someone is there who should not be there, simply send them away. This is your place of love and power. (Pause)

If you would like to, join your heart energy to theirs as you have done in our work together. Now ask, "Why are you here?" (Long Pause)

If you feel this is your guide, listen to anything they have to say. If a question feels right, ask them what they have to share with you about your Truth and your Promises. Remember, this communication can be non-verbal and totally energetic; just receive what is given. (Long Pause)

Whatever comes in this first visit is fine. Sometimes, a deep feeling of peace is the result of this meditation. That is certainly enough. There will be many more opportunities to connect with your guides. You can come here anytime. Continue to sit quietly and await any other information. (Long Pause)

If you have been blessed with a visit, thank this being for their willing-ness to help you on your journey. Take your right hand and place it over your heart. If you feel it is right for you, ask your visitor to place their hand upon your heart also. Store in your heart all the feelings of this beautiful place and this being. As you store these impressions, count backward slowly from ten to one, breathing deeply as you count, hands still on your heart. (Pause)

Whenever you are in need, stressed, or questioning, place your hand over your heart and you will return to this feeling of peace and love.

Tell your guide good-bye for now, and come back into your sacred space, into your room. Keep your eyes closed as long as you like. Remember, you can journey back to your garden anytime you desire by simply returning to a place of peace and reimaging where you were. At any time you can access this guide or others who choose to come to you simply by placing your hand over your heart and sensing your heart's garden and the peace you have created there.

When you're ready, open your eyes, breathe deeply, and write about this experience in your journal.

Music Suggestions

Should you feel you no longer need the guidance of my CDs, and this time may or may not come, make sure you use music that brings you peace and the feeling of being in sacred space. Try to be consistent with the music, for the strengthening of your connections or anchors. Anchoring your positive emotional feelings is a huge part of these jour-neys. Whether it is the use of physical anchors—as in your fingers or hands—or music, the more you use the same stimulus, the easier the process.

You may be someone who prefers silence; either way is appropriate. The only requirement is that you surround yourself with what truly honors your sacred space. If you like music, sometimes or always, Appendix II shares with you music I use personally and in my workshops. If you choose your own music, be sure it is instrumental, relaxing, heartfelt, and will continue for the entire visualization.

Further methods for receiving guidance

1) Conscious Receiving:

As you sit in your sacred space, and when you are in bed and about to go to sleep, do the **Practice for Receiving Guidance** *you have learned to access your higher self and to be calm and receptive to the sacred. If you have more time, go into the garden you created in your visualization,* **Greeting Your Personal Guides***, and make yourself available for a visit. When you are clear that it is your higher self that is open, tell your higher self that you are ready to see or feel the energy of your guides. Ask that you be given whatever you need at this time. You may have one particular guide that is with you as you begin to open to your soul's Truth and Promise.*

When you feel the presence of a guide, send out energy that says you are welcoming and grateful for the opportunity to contact your guidance. Ask for whatever is there to be given to you. Be in gratitude until you feel your time with your guide has ended for now. Write in your journal.

2) Receiving in Dreams:

When you go to bed, open to your heart energy and higher self and ask for information to come in your dreams. Ask for dreams that are specifically about your guide or guides. Do this every night, and eventually you will be in a receptive enough state to receive your guidance. If you'd like, you can do the **Greeting Your Personal Guides Visualization***, and if you fall asleep during it, you will receive guidance in that way. You may find one voice at a time, or many. Remember to keep your journal or dream book handy to write immediately when you wake up. A minute or two later, you will already be forgetting.*

It may take a little time or it may be instant, but you will have a sense of your guidance, maybe guidance you were aware of as a child but had forgotten. Sometimes you will hear a name or have a vision of a person, as I did with Jerome. Other times you may simply have a feeling of energy that is loving and comforting that you might describe as angelic. And sometimes, as it was for me with Michael, you will know the energy, and your joy will be overwhelming as you welcome those who have gone ahead into your council of guides. Remember to always express gratitude for the appearance of guidance in your life. You will come to rely on it as a true and faithful map into your future.

I've been asked many times how I know it is not just my unconscious talking to me. You will know when the communication happens. It will not be anything like your usual self-talk. The instructions, whether vocal or energetic, will be in a form or persona that is not you. Since you are asking in a spiritual setting through your higher self, nothing that is not perfect will come to you. If you feel uncomfortable or the energy feels "off", simply tell your higher self to take care of it. You will notice that the energetic vibration of the information will come in a way that you do not recognize as your daily way of receiving information. If you hear an actual voice—called clairaudience—it will be easier, but the energy of my son is familiar to me and cannot be mistaken for anyone else.

There is so much written in the books we find spiritually "normal" that says this whole process is natural. Jesus said he would be with us; we simply had to ask. He didn't say he would only come to one representative of the group. The wisdom of the creator is beyond understanding, but we can take advantage of all the aid we have been promised. Miracles did not cease when the Bible story, or the Koran, or any other religious text ended. There was not one single time in history when everything was clear. We live in the right time for us and the support of the spiritual and metaphysical is always there. We simply have to believe that and tap in.

When you have become comfortable with this process, you may find yourself referring questions to your guide/guides during the day without thinking about it. When this happens, your sacred space has enlarged to include those who wish to aid you on your path to the Truth and the Promise.

What Next?

〜☙〜

Our deepest fear is not that we are inadequate. Our deepest fear is that we are powerful beyond measure. It is our light, not our darkness, that most frightens us. We ask ourselves, 'Who am I to be brilliant, gorgeous, talented, fabulous?' Actually, who are you not to be? You are a child of God. Your playing small does not serve the world.

—Nelson Mandela, Inaugural Speech, 1994

〜☙〜

The guidance we are receiving through our personal desire and sacred intention is our birthright. When we "play small," we are defeating the purpose of our souls. If you have any negative thoughts, such as, "Why should these beings come to speak to me?" you are stopping the most natural, most healing, most loving connections in the universe. When you are comfortable with your guidance, it is time to use this wisdom and love in specific ways during your meditations and intentions. It is time to ask your guides specific questions. "What is the Promise I made before I was born? What is the Promise that was made to me? What is the Truth I must tell?" Ask these questions each time you do the meditation in your garden, each time you fall asleep, and anytime you feel the presence of guidance around you, in cards, or books. This will be ongoing for you until you have a definite knowing of your individual path. The more you practice, the sooner you will have answers.

There are other uses for meditation and visualization that I want to share with you. For example, when you are grieving or have a need to forgive or need to be released from fear, the strength and support of your higher self and your inner and outer guides will infuse the process with a depth that was not possible when you didn't acknowledge this presence. When you need healing, whether from emotional hurt or physical illness, these processes are invaluable. A healthy physical body and a healthy emotional body are excellent receptacles for guidance. Though we can receive at any time, it is easier when we are well. We will begin with healing.

It is necessary to share my journey through illness in order to make sense of the suggestions for healing. After my divorce, I had a mammogram that showed a dark spot in the upper quadrant of my left breast. In meditation, I heard that this was a wounding. My doctor sent me to a surgeon, who wanted to do immediate surgery, removing other surrounding tissue for safety. In her opinion, biopsies could be more dangerous. A second opinion recommended a biopsy followed by a full excision with removal of a gland or two to be on the safe side! I had lost two friends to breast cancer and had read essays by doctors who believed a biopsy could disturb cells that were contained and actually *increase* the spread of cancer in the body. I assumed this was the rationale behind the first doctor's approach.

Finding the right words to use when I decided to give my body a chance to heal on its own became a real struggle. Ours is not a culture that honors the intuitive. I didn't want to place myself outside the medical community, since there is much wisdom in that world. I wanted to be under the care of a medical person who would not demand that I have immediate surgery or face dire consequences. I finally found a nurse-practitioner in a doctor's office who made a contract with me. She required that I have a sonogram every six weeks, and if there was growth in the "tumor," I would immediately consent to surgery.

As soon as I had been shown the films, I began a twice daily visualization of the place in my breast. I did my usual morning ritual of yoga, prayer at the altar, calling in my guides, and then followed it with energy visualization for fifteen minutes. I imaged a ball of light rising through my feet from the center of mother earth; another shaft of light entered through the top of my head. The colors of the energy were pink for healing and purple for higher energy. I envisioned this light energy converging on the place seen in the film and wrapping it tight with healing light. Then I envisioned it growing smaller and smaller and finally disappearing. I followed this with a total chakra energy visualization, which I will share with you in the next section.

After six weeks, I had a sonogram. There was no change in what they now called a tumor rather than a dark spot—probably to scare me into following their advice. The doctor in radiology who read the film and the technician who performed the sonogram were noticeably cold and judgmental about what I was doing. Friends and family were struggling to accept that I would be unwilling to have surgery immediately, including some who were really angry with me. This is so understandable. Modern technology has invented many wonderful tools to help the sick—family and friends simply want you to be better *now.*

Not everyone should do what I did, and I am not advocating it. I am simply sharing what happened to me and how I learned to listen to my guidance. I was following a strong intuitive and guided feeling that this was the right thing for me at the time. I was convinced the stress of the past two years was the cause of this darkness growing inside. I was meditating, taking vitamins and minerals recommended by the nurse practitioner, and allowing my body to speak to me. If, at any time I had felt a change in the intuition I was receiving, I would have followed that into the surgery suite.

After another six weeks, there was a noticeable shrinkage in one section, resembling a waning moon. After the next six weeks, it was a half moon, and after the next six weeks it was no longer there. When the hospital technician gave the doctor in radiology the films, he yelled at her for giving him the wrong patient's chart. When he finally acknowledged it was mine, I asked him if he would like to know what I'd done. He turned and walked out of the room.

I may have simply been one of those lucky people whose body reabsorbs a growth. We'll never know, but I was happy to have avoided the invasion of my body that is surgery. A question that always comes up in workshops revolves around why, if we're working so hard to be good spiritual people, we are visited with tragedy and pain. This is the question of the modern world. The old world accepted it as part of the wholeness of life and never expected perfection. In his beautiful and startling poem "The Guest House," as presented by Coleman Barks, the poet Rumi addresses this issue when he says:

This being human is a guest house.
Every morning is a new arrival.
A joy, a depression, a meanness,
some momentary awareness comes as an unexpected visitor.

The poet advises us to *welcome* all that comes into ourselves, without exception, and not only that, but to be *grateful* for what comes. This is not a Western concept. We are into *accepting* with stoicism and faith; we are not into being grateful when our visitors are, as the poet says, "a crowd of sorrows who violently sweep your house empty." His absolute certainty is that all of these have been sent purposefully, not just for our own use, but as a guide to the living of his life.

If I planned on congratulating myself on the healing, which I did not since I felt it had been done through tapping in to divine intervention, this poem would have reminded me of one important thing: Rumi's view of the spiritual is the correct view. We have such limited vision where the universe is concerned. We would do well to assume *all things* that arrive on our doorstep are for our own growth and healing.

In the case of the chronic agonizing pain I developed a couple of years later, I was certainly not Rumi-like in my response. This pain was in my anus, and a literal pain-in-the-butt was not what I needed as I *sat down* to begin my next book, the novel *A Time to Reap*. If the growth in my breast was a grieving of lost possibilities and a sense of having failed to "nurture" my marriage, what was this?

I had been doing vigorous workouts, including weight lifting two to three times a week. Before that, I had been the poster child for a black belt program, where the twentysomething male instructors were determined to push the limit on what a fiftysomething woman could do. In my last test, I did forty-five minutes of movement, mostly crouching, in deep sand at the beach. That was when I awoke and called it quits. My thighs were getting as big as Arnold's! Now I was limited to a sedentary life that sometimes didn't even include sitting. And, horror of horrors, I was gaining weight rapidly.

Sitting? No. Exercising? No. Stretching? No. Crying? Yes. Body changes? Yes. In chakra energy education and many other forms of healing, the root chakra controls all feelings around family, community, and holding on to things. Losing my marriage, some of my family and friends, and my financial support were certainly root chakra issues. Bringing Lance into my circle of life also changed the dynamics between myself and others.

I *held on* to making some semblance of *normalcy* (translation: old stuff) in my daily life, continuing to help out at the family business and have contact with my ex-husband. I considered myself a good and generous role model as I transitioned into singlehood. But I forgot one important thing; I forgot to mourn. No—two things; I forgot to get angry. I could ohm all day and it wouldn't matter. There are steps that need to be taken.

The doctors (three of them) said I had hemorrhoids and only surgery could resolve it. I was told that they were so bad, I could lose bowel function after the surgery, but there was no other way. The third doctor said I needed a "hemorrhoidectomy and then an 'expansion' of your anus," since this part of my anatomy was, in his estimation, too small. Every time I was examined, the pain increased, and I was bedridden with pain medications for days. I had never experienced such excruciating pain. I had experienced hemorrhoids after the birth of my children and on rare other occasions, and this pain bore no resemblance to that pain. My intuition told me that was *not* what was going on.

I went to a highly recommended doctor/surgeon, where I was told that it was not hemorrhoids but anal fissures, tears in the fragile tissues around and in the anus. The exam had been so painful—his examination room looked like something from Dr. Strangelove with coils of metal dangling from the ceiling—that I had to ask Lance later what he had said. I felt such relief at having found the name for what I was experiencing. Name it and you can deal with it.

This doctor also said surgery was the only answer, but it wasn't always successful due to the nature of the tissues. And, yes, there were possible side effects such as loss of bowel control. I asked about natural healing, and he said it could take years and had rarely happened, in his experience. I thanked him and we went home. Later that night, he sent me pain medication to relieve what felt like invasive hot iron. I had dreams about being impaled! From that day forward I accepted my limited mobility and accepted that it would last until my body healed itself. My patience ran out when, due to unbelievable pain, I was bedridden and missed the first Thanksgiving with my children since they'd been born.

In December of 2003 Lance and I traveled to a clinic in California that was famous for healing through natural and/or complementary processes. There, the doctor confirmed the diagnosis and said he had been told by other patients that this was one of the worst pains imaginable, and the exams I had been getting had only increased the damage. He also felt there was a condition present called "pelvic spasms" resulting from stress, and my blood levels showed a definite lowered immune system, also due to stress. Did the stress cause the pain or the pain cause the stress? It didn't matter.

There was no cure, as far as he knew, but time and patience. He asked if I were willing to try the hyperbaric chamber, a method used to heal wounds, especially in diabetics. They had never used it for my issue. Of course—I would try anything at that point. He also prescribed multiple types of vitamins and minerals.

As I prepared to enter the tightly enclosed space, the nurse took my blood pressure and said I couldn't go in because it was too high. I realized I was in fear of entering that bullet-shaped tin can. But I was desperate for healing. I meditated for about fifteen minutes and she took my blood pressure again. It was normal, so I entered the hyperbaric chamber for the first time. The pain got worse after the treatment, and they had to give me a shot of morphine to stop the agony. Something major was going on here, but I was determined to give this route all I had to give. I had four treatments before I discovered they had a different type of chamber. This one was for one person and resembled a coffin, but, surprisingly, I was comfortable there. I could lie on my back instead of sitting on a metal bench. When we left the clinic after a week, I was still in pain but I felt hope. I knew the healing had begun.

Back home, I continued the meditations for relaxation and forgiveness I had begun in California. I visualized healing energy going to the place of pain, and practiced releasing all attachments to my ex-husband's life, his financial support and former friends that we had enjoyed together. It wasn't until I acknowledged my anger and disappointment that I began to get better. My plan had been to be married to the same person all my life and stay in the same house and welcome my grandchildren and, and, and…I had never accepted that old axiom that life is what happens while you're making plans.

It was not early in the process that I saw the gift in the divorce—the new life that awaited me. Later, it was not easy to uproot from Florida and go to California with Lance. It was not easy to leave the familiar comfort of my grown children and my home. It was not easy to see that my work would flourish in a climate so distant from my planned life. It was not easy to thank my ex-husband for seeing the rightness of our separation as I clung on to our familiar life. Again, as Rumi says, "…treat each guest honorably. He or she may be clearing you out for some new delight." Yes, yes, and yes.

I began acupuncture with Cheryl Thomas less than two years ago, and I believe that was the last piece of the puzzle of healing that I needed. Naturally, acupuncture is energy based, and I had finally learned the connection between my body energy and the healing energy I required from the universe. I wish I could say it happened quickly, but my entire process took over three years. I believe now that it was the culmination of a lifetime of believing that I controlled my environment. All the great teachers will tell you what a joke that is. The only thing we control is our approach to how we live, our awareness of our energy, and our perception of what happens. We are not always right about what is best for us when we are not tuned in to our higher wisdom, and adjusting to that is harder for some than others.

Sometimes I felt like giving up, but a self-scan of my body would always reveal that there had been progress. I was not in the pain I had been in before—I was experiencing "major discomfort." I was no longer taking pills for the pain. One day, less than a year ago, I knew the healing was complete. As I write this book, spending full days in my computer chair, I feel uncomfortable and have a twinge of "Oh no, not that!"

I'm working on taking that reaction out of my cells too! But now, I can *sit* in the chair. I feel healed enough to do light stretching, walking, and yoga, but my health care guides say I will not go back to weight lifting in this lifetime!

The most important lesson I learned is that illness almost always reflects a situation going on your life, or having gone on in your life, that has stored itself in your emotional body and then into your physical body. Surgery can cut it out, but learning its root is about growth and permanent healing. That, again, is the subject for whole books, and there are many good ones out there if this subject interests you. (See Appendix II.)

I repeat that I am not medically trained and would never advise you about a particular illness. As I described, I followed the medical smorgasbord myself but then chose from the menu what worked for me. You *must*, in this growth of the spiritual life, tune in to your own guidance and intuition. Sometimes that will lead you to a wonderful doctor or hospital. There are many formerly mainstream hospitals that are now using alternative methods of healing as well as Eastern and Western methods. Scripps clinic in La Jolla, only a few miles from where I now live, is an example. The Whitaker Center in Newport Beach, California, is another. Even these have a long way to go in respecting your awareness of your body.

Be persistent, trust your inner signals, and advocate for yourself. Any healing modalities you add from your own knowing can only help in the process. There are many and varied instant health and longevity hucksters out there, as well as honestly effective products. If you are approached with magic elixir type stories, trust your own intuition and consult with others you trust before embarking on anyone else's journey. In the meantime, your healing process cannot be undermined when you are using meditation and visualization and your own body energy to heal.

Chakra Information

It will help to do healing work to visualize the location and color of the chakras. This is a name given in Eastern training to the energy centers of the body. These energy centers are demonstrated in modern Western medicine through the use of EKGs, EEGs, etc. Chakra visualizations are available in many books. For our purposes here, it is enough to know that the energy in your body flows through centers. These are the centers used in acupuncture and other forms of energy healing. The main centers range in a line from above your head to the pelvic floor. These centers are visualized, in many circles, as cone shaped, with the narrow end attached at the spinal column and the open end a short distance in front of the body. The one above the head has its point at the skull and the opening above the head to receive higher energy; the pelvic chakra, or root, has the point up and the opening toward the ground, to receive earth energies.

I like knowing the colors, as it helps me to visualize the energy as a color going into the places that need energy. I give you a couple of pieces of information that can help you to identify the emotional issues that can be affecting your health in certain areas. The chakra centers are as follows.

First or Root Chakra
Location: Base of spine
Issues: Survival, stability, acceptance, self-preservation, safety
Color: Red

Identity: Physical/Tribal
Negative Emotion: Fear

Second or Sacral Chakra
Location: Lower Abdomen
Issues: Sexuality, emotions, finances, ethics
Color: Orange
Identity: Emotional
Negative Emotion: Guilt

Third or Solar Plexus Chakra
Location: Solar Plexus
Issues: Power, self-esteem, self-image, energy, responsibility, will
Color: Yellow
Identity: Ego Identity
Negative Emotion: Shame

Fourth or Heart Chakra
Location: Chest, heart
Issues: Love, forgiveness, relationship, depression, loneliness
Colors: Green/Pink
Identity: Social Identity
Negative Emotion: Grief

Fifth or Throat Chakra
Location: Throat
Issues: Communication, self-expression, self-discipline, speaking out, truth
Colors: Blue, light blue, turquoise
Identity: Creative
Negative Emotion: Lies

Sixth or Third Eye Chakra
Location: Center of the forehead
Issues: Intuition, imagination, ability to see one's life clearly, use of mind/intellect
Color: Indigo

Identity: Archetypal
Negative Emotion: Illusion

Seventh or Crown Chakra
Location: The crown of the skull
Issues: Awareness, spiritual search for meaning, grace, spiritual awakening
Colors: Purple, white, gold, silver
Identity: Universal
Negative Emotion: Thought

Be sure you do the following visualization, **Track 5 on the CD: Healing Visualization I** before doing the next exercise in the book, **Chakra Rainbow Guided Visualization II,** which is not on the CD.

Also, please, *review the chakra area information prior to listening to the CD or your own recording.* Find the area nearest to your physical discomfort or illness, or the negative emotion you are feeling. Imagine where it is—exactly or as close as you can determine—in your body. When you are sure, note the color associated with this place in your body and continue.

Healing Meditation
Visualization I

This meditation is track 5 on the CD
Time: 11 minutes, 15 seconds plus time for journaling

Be sure you have reviewed the chakra information in the book, prior to doing this visualization.

Relax in whatever way has become familiar to you, preferably in a quiet place you call sacred where you won't be interrupted. Begin the CD or your own recording.

If you can, take off your shoes. Place your feet flat on the floor— especially the ball of your foot—this is an acupressure/acupuncture point that takes in direct energy. Let your hands rest loosely in your lap and hold your spine as straight as possible. If you are in pain, allow your body to take the least stressful position; even lying in bed is fine.

Close your eyes. Breathe deeply, filling your abdomen and lungs to their fullest point. Breathe out, letting your abdomen relax toward your backbone. Do this five times. If you have practiced going to your peaceful place by pressing your thumb and forefinger together, do so now. Breathe. (Pause)

Go into your heart's garden, where you will see several seats in a circle. Take a seat and ask for your personal guides that are healers for you to come and sit with you in the garden circle. If you ask, they will come. Ask them to

179

assist in your healing. Sense their presence as they strengthen your energy. (Pause)

Remember to breathe deeply. Visualize your body and focus on the place you want to heal. See it physically or visualize it as an object in the correct place in your body, or feel it as energy or heat. This is the place you want to penetrate and saturate with good light-force energy. You are healing with love and light. If you can, see or sense the color, using your chakra knowledge, of the injury/illness/discomfort. Breathe deeply. (Pause)

Now, see, feel, or sense a large ball of energy beneath the surface of the floor or ground, and color it the color of the chakra closest to the place you desire to heal, or if another color comes to you intuitively, use what feels right to you. Breathe. (Pause)

Concentrate, ask for support from your guides, and raise this ball of energy through the floor into your feet. Be aware of any sensations the energy gives you. (Pause and breathe.)

The ball of colored energy is now rising through your legs, pausing at the base of your spine and then, slowly, rising up your spine. Remember to breathe deep as you guide this energy. (Pause)

Using all your powers of concentration, slow the energy down and see it expanding into your body, filling all of the major organs...the bones...and muscles... Breathe it in. Your whole body is now saturated in healing, light-force energy. (Pause)

Now, condense the mass of energy back into a ball, and with the help of your guides, bring it slowly to the place where you desire healing. Let it vibrate in that space as you breathe deeply. Speak silently of your desire for, and acceptance of, healing. Breathe comfortably. **See Yourself Healed!** *(Long Pause)*

Using all your powers of concentration, and your breath, take your time and bring the energy upward until it rises out of your body at your crown, hovering there. (Long Pause)

When you have finished that process, let the ball of energy above your head descend and wash down through your body, slowly, from your crown to your feet and then down into the earth, back to its source. Again, ask your guides to help guide the energy. Take your time, do this slowly and deliberately, breathing deeply. (Pause)

Sit quietly and notice any feelings, emotional or physical, that are in your body after washing it with your light-force energy. (Pause)

It is nearly time to leave the garden. Give thanks and gratitude for your own gifts of healing, the intelligence of your body, and whomever or whatever energies you were aware of that assisted you. (Pause)

When you have finished, open your eyes and immediately write everything you remember in your journal.

The journal writing is very important! Note how your guidance felt, what the energy felt like in your body, how relaxed you were (or were not.) As you continue to practice the healing work on a daily basis, note the changes in your physical and emotional bodies after the visualization.

As with all the other processes, these take time and repetition to become a familiar part of your life. Once you have mastered them, and this usually involves modifying them to meet your own personality needs, you will naturally go to them when needed. When I say modify, I am reminding you that I created these to work for *me*! It was *my* intuition and knowing that said, "Do this." If you are in the midst of visualization and something comes in and feels right to you, do it. These are guidelines, not rules. The only rule, as I've said, is that it feels true and right for you in your body and intuition. When it does not, let it go. Let me know what you are finding, and I will share it with others—with your permission, of course.

Heart, Tell Me
Writing Exercise for Healing

Before you go to the next visualization, please take out your journal. Read what you wrote after doing the Healing Visualization I. Now, close your eyes and see again the part of you that you want to heal. Take your time; open your eyes when you see the place that calls out for healing or comfort.

In the Dialogue Section of this book, I heard, and wrote, two short pieces to me from two parts of myself; my body and, specifically, my heart. The heart piece began: **Heart, Tell Me...**

It is sometimes easiest to begin with the body itself. Go through from head to toe or work on a specific place.

Body, Tell Me...

*When you have isolated the part of you that you want to heal, ask the question I asked, naming your particular area of pain, illness, or discomfort. Let the pen move across the page without stopping, writing down the communication from your body to yourself. Once you have a sense of your body as a physical, energetic, and emotional part of you that **wants** you to know how it is, truly, the healing will have a personal connection that it does not have when you see, for instance, your heart in an x-ray.*

It helps to read this message from your emotional intelligent body self on a regular basis, and then add comments in your journal as things change.

The next healing visualization, **Healing Meditation II: Chakra Rainbow,** is also based on the chakra centers. It is both specific and used for a general body tune-up. This can take as little as fifteen minutes for one chakra—as you experienced in **Healing Visualization I, Track 5** on the CD—or as long as you want based on doing a full chakra cleansing (this is not on the CD). The basic process is the same, but you will go through all the chakras from base to higher self in a consecutive procedure. Allow plenty of time if you want to do the whole "rainbow" process.

Don't make this complicated. Repeat the healing visualization on the CD as many times as it takes to become a natural part of your being. Then, try reading through the following chakra healing several times. (Record it in your own voice if you would like, or have a friend or healer you are working with read it to you.) Begin with one color, one chakra, and one process. After a few weeks you will be doing the entire chakra cleansing whenever you want without even thinking about it. I recommend, highly, that you copy this part of the book and put it in a binder and purchase and use tracks 6, 7, and 8 of *Solace* by Michael Hoppé. Every time you use the same music, it acts as an impetus to the healing process.

Healing Meditation
Visualization II

Chakra Rainbow

Visualization not on CD
Time: Approximately 10 minutes per chakra (to be done one at a time or all at one sitting.)

This is a process that I use at least once a week, whether I have an issue or not. I think of it as a tune-up! As before, review the chakra information if you don't know it already. Play a peaceful meditative piece of music if you plan to use music. You will need to practice this for a while before it becomes second nature.

You know what to do now—relax, bring in your sacred space, close your eyes, and begin deep breathing.

Sit with your feet, especially the balls of the feet, flat on the floor, your hands loose in your lap, your spine straight. Always, this is if no pain is involved. Otherwise, lying in bed is fine. Continue to breathe deeply throughout this visualization. Always come back to your breath.

There is a ball of energy gathered under your feet. Raise it slowly up your legs, stopping to massage the joints of your knees, the muscles of your thighs. Breathe deeply as you do this. (Pause)

We will begin with the base chakra. Bring this energy to the base of your spine and saturate it with brilliant red. Turn it into a spinning vortex of

184

energy at the base of your spine, and guide it into the lower part of your body. Breathe deeply. (Pause)

Slowly raise the red energy up through the middle of your body, through the sexual organs, the reproductive organs, the elimination system, the bladder, liver, gall bladder, and all other organs in your lower body and on up into the stomach and digestive tract. (Pause)

As you breathe, the red base chakra energy continues to swirl upward through your chest, energizing your heart, lungs, and rising into your throat. Breathe. (Pause)

Now, bring the liquid red energy up your throat and into your mouth, bathing the tongue, gums, sinuses, and inner ear with healing energy. (Pause)

Raise the energy up through the forehead into the cranium and gently wash the brain with energizing red liquid healing. Breathe, breathe. (Pause)

Now, visualize an opening in the top of your head and allow the red energy to rise out the top like a fountain, flowing down your body like red water, front and back, until it pools at your feet. (Pause)

Absorb the energy back into the root chakra, and when you're ready, open your eyes and come back into the room.*

Write about this experience in your journal right away. Note what you noticed in different areas of your body.

* Note: After you have done this once or twice, you will not absorb the energy back into the chakra, but leave it around your body. Then, you will continue to add each chakra color in the same way you did above, until you have a rainbow around your body. In other words, after the red (root) chakra energy has come down to your feet in the last segment, you will go to your orange (belly) chakra, begin that color spinning, and go through the entire process again. When the orange flows down the outside of your body, it will be over the red. The same will be true when you do the yellow color from your solar plexus (just below the diaphragm)—you will go through the whole process and then have three colors around your body like a rainbow, and so on. After a complete chakra rainbow has been created around your body, you will keep it there as you go through your day. It will be an energetic presence in your daily work and life. Since this process takes so much longer, you will probably use the one energy/color most needed at any particular time. I encourage you, however, to get to the point where you do the entire rainbow at least once a week. It is so physically energizing and was no small part of my healing!

Music Suggestion: Again, I recommend that you use Michael Hoppé's CD, *Solace*, track 8, called "Nimbus." This is the music beneath my voice as I guided you through the first healing visualization. Once you learn the process, you can do all the chakras, or one at a time, using this music.

Forgiveness: The Sacred Act

Another side of healing is forgiveness. Carrying anger and hurt creates great strain on the physical body, so it is for our own good that we learn to forgive. However, it is so important to know, and cannot be stressed too often, that forgiveness is not forgetting. For many reasons, including being careful not to make the same choices again, we can use past traumas as guidelines—the body's early warning systems.

There are many people in certain programs who are told they must say "I'm sorry," or "I accept this as part of my learning path," and then, they rationalize, they will be relieved of responsibility for their actions. This is often true even when the program doesn't tell them it's true. Some who have been wounded want a little more than those words— they want true emotional awareness of the harm that was done to them. Then they can forgive.

Those who have been grievously wronged may come to all sorts of conclusions through therapy, religion, or other means. They may be convinced to say that it is all okay because it was part of their growth process. I myself have said that about certain traumas in my own life. That does *not* eliminate the fact that they happened, the suffering occurred, and sometimes physical harm was done. We have a memory which can be *separated* from the emotional trauma of the memory, but what was done was still done. There are ways to separate the happening from the emotion, including *Somatic Intuitive Training*, but I am going to lead you through a process that will help you disconnect from issues and people that cause you pain. That is the first step.

186

On the other side of the issue, coming to forgiveness from a lofty peak of "I forgive you because I was right and you were wrong" won't work either. This forgiveness thing is very tricky. It must be entered into with only one thing in mind. "I will be better off when I am not attached to this person through my wounding." It isn't about them—it's about you. It's about you having a healthy body, mind, and spirit unencumbered by the baggage of another soul. It's about being free. It truly does not matter how deep and how grievous the harm was. It still needs to be eliminated from your cells. Let's begin.

The following visualization is for the purpose of disconnecting you from someone or something you wish to be disconnected from physically and emotionally. An example of a "thing" is an organization or a teaching. Sit quietly in your sacred space. Assure yourself that you will be uninterrupted for the time you need on this issue. Make sure your phone is off. In order to be effective, this is a process that needs to go from start to end without leaving any part undone. Don't forget to use all of your tools, since forgiveness is one of the most difficult processes for some people and requires support. Light a candle and sage your space, if you have sage available.

Since you have created the garden in your heart as a safe place, it would be good to close your eyes and go there to re-establish these feelings before you begin this process. Use all your senses to experience this wonderful, peaceful place—this sanctuary in your heart. Once you have a feeling of peace and calm, add the pressure of your finger anchors to complete the feeling.

Forgiveness
A Guided Visualization

This is track 6 on the CD

Time: 9 minutes, 17 seconds (remember to leave additional time for journaling. This is especially important in the forgiveness work.)

Part One: Someone or something you want to forgive and remove from your life. Do not complete this process if you want the person to stay in your life. Read the meditation first and note when to stop.

Begin the CD or your recording. See yourself seated in your wonderful heart garden. Breathe deeply, eyes closed, inhaling the scents of your garden, hearing the sounds of birds or chimes or falling water. Bring all of this into your body's cells and organs on your breath. Continue to breathe deeply for a few moments. (Pause)

As you continue to breathe deeply, find the person you need to forgive and want to go from your life. Without bringing them into your garden, imagine them where they are. If they have already gone from this world, imagine them where you think *they are. (Pause)*

There are cords coming from your body and connecting to this other person's body. See, feel, or sense these cords any way you like: webs, ropes, telephone wires, or pure energy. Breathe deeply and relax, seeing or sensing these connections as powerfully as possible. (Pause)

Now, go to your higher self, as you've practiced for some time, and ask your higher self to communicate with the other person's higher self. Breathe deeply until you hear a "yes" from your intuition that this connection has occurred. (Pause)

Speak from your higher self to the other person's higher self—all is accepted at that level. You do not have an issue with this person outside of the physical world, or in your higher self. The ego does not exist there. Say the following words, and follow them with whatever you want to say. Remember to breathe deeply and take your time.

"I forgive you for ——————————," (name what it is that has wounded you). Now, say what you need to say. Breathe deeply. (Long Pause)

See or sense the cords between you and the other person disconnecting and falling away. As they go, scan your body for anywhere else you may be connected to this person and let it go. Breathe deeply into those places where you were attached. Experience total peace as the cords of attachment to the person and the hurt disappear and your body heals where you were attached. (Long Pause) (Take six deep breaths.)

Imagine the person again, where they are, completely whole and separate. Now, as you watch, the person begins to move away from your vision, becoming smaller and smaller until all you see is a small dot of energy where they were, and then, nothing. You can also feel this as energy moving away from you. (Pause) Breathe as they go.

Keep your eyes closed and continue to breathe in your garden heart center. Thank your higher self for speaking for you. Stay in this quiet, calm space as long as you want, breathing deeply and feeling the energy flow through all the cells of your body. When you're ready, open your eyes.

Write in your journal about this as soon as you finish. If at anytime you feel there is still a connection, repeat this process until there is no energy between you.

Forgiveness Part II
Forgiving and Keeping the Person in Your Life

The process of forgiveness is one of the most freeing tools you will ever use in your life. The above visualization can be changed to forgive a person who has deeply hurt you, but that you want to keep in your life for whatever reason. Begin with the Guided Visualization, Part One, but stop when you are directed to make the person smaller and smaller until they disappear from your life. Go to the last paragraph once you have released all the connections. Once you are familiar with the process, I recommend using the Michael Hoppé CD Solace, track 6, "Renouncement," which is the music I used in the guided portion. It will continue to reinforce the forgiveness as the music becomes more and more a part of that path. I recommend that you do the following as often as possible.

Forgiveness Part III
A Brief Meditation on Forgiveness

An alternate meditation can be done in the morning for only a few minutes, while the visualization is a deeper work on more specific matters. It is also part of our Truth that we hold many grievances against ourselves. This meditation can be used daily to name and forgive that pain we have caused to ourselves; those judgments that we make against our bodies, our minds, our abilities, our...you fill in the blank. It is not always necessary to name the wound we have inflicted on ourselves, but sometimes it helps to do so. I will leave a space in the meditation for you if you find it appropriate.

You may sit or lay down for this meditation. I recommend that you use the music you use for the forgiveness visualization, as it will reinforce the process when used often. (It will become an anchor, just like your finger anchors.) Simply hearing the music will begin the process of forgiveness. Do this short meditation daily, if possible, and aloud if you are able.

Go to your heart garden, press your fingers together, and breathe deeply for a few moments. Lay your hands on your heart area, and speak the following words, either aloud or in your heart.

"I ask for the presence of my guides (name them here, if you have done the work to access your guides) and any other guidance that will help me to reach total forgiveness in my life. (Pause)

191

"I wish to be free of judgment, free of the resentment I carry, and free of the burden of blame. I surround myself with the white light of pure blessing. (Pause) (Breathe.)

"Today, I forgive others and/or myself for any pain, intentional or accidental, that has taken place between us. Specifically, I ask forgiveness of _____ for _____ and I give forgiveness to _____ for _____. (Pause) (Breathe deeply.)

"I am grateful for these moments, and I ask that the feelings of calm and peace stay with me throughout this day, and that I go to my highest self whenever hurt or judgment impact my life." (Pause)

As always, feel free to edit, add to, or replace these meditations with your own words or actions that might be more comfortable for you. The most important part of the process is remembering that each word carries energy—forgiveness, blessing, and gratitude are wonderful positive energy words. This is your life, your path, and your choice—always. My work is simply a guideline.

Grief Work

None of us get through this life without grieving, unless we have no human feelings. Loss is all around us, personally and globally. When I work with women who are going through menopause, we concentrate on the parts of them that are grieving. Sometimes, as one woman said, it is as simple as losing the ability to swing your hair from side to side. Our hair symbolizes youth and sexual attractiveness, and we take it for granted when we are young. As we age, and begin to see changes in the thickness and shine of our hair, this is a loss. Flexibility is another part of us that we take for granted until we start to lose it. Even the loss of sexual lubrication, though replaceable, is a reminder to some women that they are no longer who they once were.

First of all, I tell them that there are many exercise programs and vitamin supplements that will help them with hair, sexuality, nails, and bones, but that is not what these things are symbolic of; they are symbols of our young selves that have, literally, died to us. We are being birthed into another self. We can't do that comfortably without grieving the loss of our familiar other self.

This is the basic grieving we must do before we grieve the larger losses, like the death of friends, parents, other relatives, and sometimes, God forbid, our children. And then there is the death of our world as we know it, through changes in our neighborhoods, cities, and climate; the total impersonality of modern war; and the growth of global disaster and government. We are definitely generations that are being challenged to find the light in the darkness. It is a challenge and a gift.

Please don't find anything you grieve trivial, and don't compare it to someone else's grieving. There is no measurement. What we feel is our truth—it is valid, no matter what. To find our path, our Promises, and our Truth is to shine light into the darkness and refuse to submit. Coming to terms with our grief is the first step after forgiveness and it requires the inner courage of a Grail searcher. As I said earlier, we are equal to the task: in fact, we were born for it.

I have included a track on the CD titled "Pie Jesu" by Michael Hoppé, vocals by Heidi Fielding and Dwain Briggs. The work was written by Michael for the memorial service of his wife's mother. I have found it to be profoundly moving when clients are doing grief work. It was healing for me as I grieved the death of my son, many years later. For that reason, I am not reading the meditation, but asking you to read and practice the process, using "Pie Jesu" as background when you are doing either of the grief meditations presented on the page. I am grateful to Michael for his generous gift of this music.

This work is best when done with another, and even better when done in a group. It is very difficult to do alone. If you don't have a close friend or family member who is willing to partner with you, and you don't belong to a women's group that would be willing to try this exercise, skip this step and go to the *Grieving Exercise: You are Alone* that follows. This is an extremely powerful tool, and I urge you to find a way to do it with a partner.

Grieving
A Guided Visualization

Information for this meditation is found on track 7, and music on track 8 on the CD. You will need to study the process.

Time: 4 minutes. Take additional time for journaling—repeat the track as often as you need. Grieving is personal and takes as much time as it takes.

Listen to track 7 and let the CD go on to track 8. Otherwise, play a CD that has soulful, slow, and meditative music. Sit in a chair where you can be comfortable, across from another person in a chair. Be as close to one another as possible, since, in a few moments, you will be holding your arm up for a long period of time.

Sometimes, having one chair pulled up to the right side of the other (right side to right side, your knees beside your partner's hips) is helpful, or you can sit to the side of a table with your elbows propped.

Put on the CD and set it to repeat, if possible.

Breathe deeply, at least five times. Look into the eyes of the other person and see their soul self; the eyes are the seat of the soul. Breathe deeply. (Pause for a moment.)

Close your eyes. Ask, silently, for any guides who are available to help you with this process. (Pause) Breathe slowly and evenly, at least five times. (Pause)

Now, begin to imagine violet energy shimmering around your body and between you and your partner. Breathe deeply. Begin to see the energy going out in the direction of your partner, at the same time it surrounds your body. Breathe. Now, consciously, send the energy to each other, visualizing it as shimmering violet energy going from heart to heart.

Place your right hand on your partner's chest, above the heart. Have them do the same. Close your eyes. Relax and breathe deeply. Visualize your partner's heart, and find the places where grief is stored. You will know. Breathe. As you breathe in and out, send the healing energy, with the help of your guidance, into the places where your partner is grieving, and wash it clean. Continue to hold this intention with your hand on your partner's heart until the music comes to an end. Breathe, breathe.

When the music ends, slowly remove your hand and open your eyes when you are ready. Write in your journals everything that you felt and experienced. Replay "Pie Jesu" while you're writing. When you're finished, talk to your partner, or the group, about the experience.

Grieving Exercise
You Are Alone

Tracks 7 and 8 on the CD

Time: 4 minutes plus writing time

You will need to read this several times until you have it in your mind. Keep it nearby for guidance until you are sure of your path. Set *"Pie Jesu," or music you have chosen,* so that it repeats if necessary. Make sure you will have total quiet, no interruptions, for at least fifteen minutes.

Hopefully you have an altar now, and can light a candle, burn sage, or incense. Sit quietly, feet flat on the floor, in a comfortable, peaceful space. As always, if you are unwell or unable to sit, lie down and be as comfortable as possible.

Close your eyes. Bring together all the meditative tools you have learned so far—the garden, the pressure of your fingers, your beautiful, peace-filled memories—and sit quietly as you recall them. Breathe deeply. Take all the time you need.

When you're ready, bring into your space any guides, angels, protectors that you feel can help you on the journey to release the grief from your body. You are not meant to be alone.

Picture your body surrounded with violet colored light. Continue to breathe deeply.

Bring the violet light into your body, filling your head, your throat, your heart, and your stomach with vibrating light. Breathe it in, deeply.

Cross your hands over your heart. Call on your knowing, though you probably already know, to tell you what you need to grieve before you can be completely healthy. This can be a real death, a loss of a marriage or a job, a health issue that causes you to grieve the loss of some ability—anything, including losses due to aging or moving or a natural disaster that has changed your life. Breathe.

Find the place in your body where you feel that grief. Just be aware of your entire body. Scan it visually or energetically and find where there is discomfort. Breathe!

When you have found the place, move the violet light there and imagine that your hands, still crossed over your heart, are sending white light into your body. Feel the warmth and compassion of your wisdom and intuition, along with that of your guides, flowing into the place in your body where you feel the grief. Breathe.

If you feel the need, speak to whoever or whatever it is you are grieving. Say how you feel and why. Take all the time you need. There is no right or wrong response. Tears are often the result of getting in touch with your grieving. Remember to breathe deeply.

When you are ready, move the energy through your body and down through your feet, sending the grief into Mother Earth to be transformed. Breathe and thank any help that you had in this process, and thank yourself for the courage it took to face your grief.

When you're ready, open your eyes.

There is rarely only one thing we grieve, but one at a time is enough. Write about this in your journal, and wait at least a week before you choose to do this process again.

Releasing Our Genetic Pain

The most important thing we can do after clearing some of our negative emotions, stored as energy in our cells, is to take the big step of changing our genetic memory. It has been documented that we store memory, just as we store eye color, hair color, and temperament, from our ancestors. For example: she has Aunt Mary's temper. But we also contain fear and anger that was felt by everyone from our mother on back, based on our creation as women. Psychiatrists often work with women who learned fear in the womb from fear experienced by their mothers during pregnancy. The only way to change our cellular pain is to change our cells. This the body does daily, but it always replicates what was in the previous cell. By removing the emotion from the cells, the new cells will not contain the previous memory of pain, negation, or sadness.

The most useful and amazing gift we can give to ourselves and our female ancestors is to honor their struggles; recognize their frustration, fear, and hurt; and free them and ourselves from the burden of history. Step one is that we must first be aware of that history, or we cannot know what it is we are releasing. Please read the timeline in Appendix I before you do the following visualizations. Take into your mind and heart the fact that these things happened to your relatives, your blood kin, and those who dreamed of you. Feeling these emotions will help you to identify them and prepare you to release them.

199

Once you have done this, simply by reading and understanding the Timeline, you will be ready to go back and visit your ancestor or ancestors on your mother's or father's side and tell them that you understand, and that you give them the honor and recognition they deserve. Prepare yourself to travel to where they are, using *Sacred Feminine Visioning*—my version of Time Dimension Therapy.

To begin, you must be able to go deeply inside yourself and know that there is a thread running through you, back through your family, to first woman. It is actually a pipeline, with information running through it from generation to generation, each of us accumulating more of the past in our emotional and physical bodies. Scientifically, we know this is true. Emotionally and logically, we must accept it. Going to your higher self will help you to leave your doubts behind.

There is a whole world of study, in physics, molecular biology, and other areas, that discusses the parallel and quantum nature of time. There is no room in this book for that work, and I'm not qualified to teach it, but I urge you to read Deepak Chopra—the man I call the "Great Translator"—for a version of this work that even I can understand. Many others, such as Greg Braden and Bruce Lipton, have also written well about this subject. Michio Kaku, professor of physics, has a wonderful book I cite in Appendix II. There is no lack of teachers. Suffice it to say that if you touch the shoulder of a woman in the year 1311, she may feel you. And the déjà vu that we frequently encounter, or the little shivers that tell us someone is there, may be felt by us from the past or the future.

The first step is to grieve what we have learned and forgive those involved. When you are ready to do so, do the **Grieving Process** work with the history of women. Once you have done that, you can follow it with the **Forgiveness Exercises**. This is another reason that the grieving is done in a pairing or a group. It is a much more powerful process that way. In a group, you can read the Timeline of History and then choose all or part of it as a grieving intention.

After you have done these steps, it will be time to do the process that follows, Sacred Feminine Visualization.

Sacred Feminine
Visualization and Time Dimension Work

You will need to read this several times before you do the practice, since your eyes will be closed in the later portion. Practice finding the path with your eyes open several times before going to Part II.

Part I

First, I ask you to stand and visualize yourself on a path. Give the path substance; is it brick, stone, dirt, marble, or even shell?

Locate your past on the path and visualize where your future is. (In other words, you are standing on a path. If you want to go forward, where is the path? If you want to go back to where you were, where is the path?) Do this quickly, it will be natural. Don't think about it too much.

For most people, the past is behind them and the future in front of them and they are right on the path, looking into the future.

With others, if they hold out their arms in a V, the left part of the V is the past, the right is the future, and they are standing right at the point.

Be sure which is your way of seeing, before moving on to Part II.

Part II

Close your eyes. Breathe deeply. Stand quietly and firmly on your path. Then, turn slowly, and without opening your eyes, face your past. With your inner wisdom, see down the path of your past—or feel it energetically.

Slowly, with all the powers of your intention, imagine your body rising above the path. Visualize your path into the past for a moment or two, then, breathing deeply, turn back to the present and float there a moment. Turn and face your future, eyes still closed. Stay there a moment and then slowly return to earth, sit in a chair, your feet on the floor.

Practice rising and floating, with your eyes closed, several times, and when you are comfortable doing this, it will be time to take the journey on the CD.

Before beginning the next exercise, you will have read the Timeline of Truth and practiced the prior exercise for finding your past and future paths.

The purpose is to honor the lives of all of your ancestors by connecting with one in particular and acknowledging how difficult her life was and how much you appreciate her sacrifice. Only by doing this will you remove the accumulation of genetic suffering from your own cells. Remember that the energy and power of your unconscious mind is in charge of this journey. This is sacred work, and your mind and body can do nothing without your permission. This is a heart-centered visualization, motivated by compassion and love for those who came before us and suffered, in most cases, the difficult life of a woman of her time. Do not rush. Be sure you have at least twenty minutes, preferably more.

Honoring Your Female Ancestors
Visualization

This visualization is track 9 on the CD
Time: 13 minutes, 36 seconds, plus time to journal

Sit comfortably. Begin the CD or your recording. Close your eyes. Take a deep breath, and hold it. Now, exhale through your mouth. Another deep breath, feel your belly swell with your life force energy; now exhale through your mouth. One more time; inhale—hold—exhale through your mouth. Cross your hands lightly over your heart and enter your heart's garden once more. Feel again the sweet air, smell the fresh air—whatever is real for you. Breathe. (Pause)

See two paths, one leading in and one leading out of your garden—they are connected where you are. As you practiced earlier, in your imagination, **slowly** *rise and hover above the path. Sense one continuous path flowing through the past, present, and future. Breathe. (Pause)*

As you rise, slowly and gently turn your body toward the past and begin to float backward in time—stay above your path. As you float above this path, past your younger self, past your birth, you will see or sense the women of your extended family below you; you may see or sense the energy of your mother, her mother, and her mother; or you may just have a feeling for the numbers of women whose genes make you who you are today. This is an unbroken line—

*your entire female lineage back to the beginning of time. Continue to float
back, slowly,* above your path. *Let your unconscious roam. Whoever wants to
come up, will. As they do, acknowledge and honor them. You are looking for
one particular woman. Breathe. (Pause)*

*Stay aware of your own body. Let your body energy search below
you until you sense a pull, a comfortable knowing that one individual
woman needs your presence. When you know it is time, go slowly and
lightly, as if you had a parachute on your back, down onto the path.
You will know if you are in the right place. You'll sense it in your body.
Breathe. (Long Pause)*

*Usually, you'll feel like you're in a movie. When you settle into that place
and time, look around you to get a sense of where you are. If you're outside,
note the sounds, the terrain, the feel of the air—what it smells like. What trees
grow here?*

*Do you feel this place is familiar to you? If you are inside, note the walls, the
floors, the smells, and sounds. Breathe deeply. Is anyone else around? (Pause)*

*If you are meant to be here, you will see or sense her now. Does she remind
you of anyone? Her eyes? Her smile? Her hair? Her energy? Notice details;
then ask your higher self if you already know who she is. (Pause)*

*Now, approach her slowly and join your heart energy to hers. Speak to
her through your higher self and your heart. You know how. Do this now, letting your wisdom and intuition guide your words. If you are not comfortable
speaking to her, simply be there with her. Breathe. (Pause)*

If you don't already know, and would like to, ask her who she is. (Pause)

*Does she have something to tell you? Take your time here. If it is
comfortable for you, relax and allow her to speak to you through your higher
self connection. If not, just be with her. Breathe. (Pause)*

*If she does not respond, simply feel her energetic presence. That may be all
that is necessary in this time and place. (Long Pause)*

*You are going to leave here soon. Stay connected to her until you are ready
to leave. Reach out and touch her on the shoulder or wherever feels appropriate to you. Feel each other physically across the years. Take your time. This is
true soul work. Then, tell her good-bye. Memorize what you can about her.
Breathe deeply. (Pause)*

*Picture yourself rising back up above your path, your ancestor or guide
growing smaller below you.*

Turn toward the present. You have one more task. As you float slowly back to this time and place, shine your loving light and gratitude down onto the path, touching each woman of your line with Grace as you sense her energy. Ask for help with this from your guides, or if you are too tired, leave it until the next time you go on this journey. Go slowly, slowly, until you are above the present, then softly drift down into your chair in your room. Take the time you need to come back, breathing deeply and steadily.

When you're ready, open your eyes and quietly write whatever you feel you want to remember of this experience in your journal.

Know that you can return anytime you want to by putting your hands on your heart, turning on this CD or other music, and stepping into your heart's garden.

Anytime you need advice or are in a stressful situation, you can place your hands over your heart—lower if you're at a table or desk— and these feelings of peace and wisdom will return to you.

Celebrating the Past
and Future

This visualization is not on the CD. Play joyful celebratory music as you do the following process. (Example: *Chariots of Fire*, soundtrack, Vangelis Papathanassiou.)
Time: 15 minutes plus journaling.

Go into your sacred space, making sure you won't be disturbed. Sit quietly and close your eyes. Later, you might want to do this with friends.

Breathe deeply, taking your time. You have all the time you need. Breathe and absorb the music. (Pause)

Visualize yourself walking into a lovely meadow. Crossing the meadow is your path—the path that leads to the past and the future. See what it is made of, or sense its material as you step upon it. You are exactly at "now" on your path, and imagine that it is in the center of the meadow. As far as your imagination can see, or sense, there are flowers, waving grasses, and shade trees. Maybe there are mountains in the distance, or a stream bisecting it. This is your meadow. Make it as you wish it to be. Breathe. (Pause)

In your imagination, see your path extending far into the past and out into the future. As you watch, small figures are moving toward you along the path, growing as they near you, and you see that it is the long line of your ancestors coming to gather with you in the meadow. Just relax, and watch them come. Some are singing, some carrying food, others have small musical instruments like tambourines and drums. Whatever they want to show you, relax and enjoy it. Breathe. (Pause)

Now turn your attention to the future. You see the same phenomenon happening. Women from the future, young and old, are coming down the path to the present—hundreds, or even thousands of them. All of them are mingling and gathering with the women from the past, greeting them, asking them questions, comparing skin, eyes, hair. (Pause)

Go into the throng of women. Choose someone you want to visit with, then another. Take your time. (Pause)

You begin to notice something strange—every woman has a darkness rising from her body, rising above her head and joining the darkness from all the other women that is gathering in the sky. It looks like thunderclouds piling up before a storm. At the same time, the women look lighter, happier, and younger. They are making circles within circles and beginning to dance, as the wind comes up and whips their clothes around. Some of the younger women are whirling in place, the dark wisps disappearing above their heads turning gray, then white, and then gone.

Lightning flashes through the clouds, turning the blackness silver, then golden, then a peach color; the edges soften, rays of sunshine shooting out from behind the clouds. This accumulation of grief, sadness, anger, and despair has erupted into a storm in the heavens, transformed by the beautiful spiritual love of the women in the meadow. This legacy will not be passed on to the next generations of women. It has been exposed and cleansed in the power of this gathering.

There has never been such an auspicious gathering of women. Feel the sense of family; hear the joy; sense the fresh clean air washed clear of pain.

When you are ready, watch as the women walk back along their paths, back to the past or the future. All of you know you can gather any time you want, simply by holding the intention and putting your energy there. It is such a joy to see, hear, and feel the great network of women that join you to past and future. This is a gift of time and energy that comes directly from your wisdom and intuition and the wisdom of all women back to the beginning of time. (Pause)

Open your eyes, come back into the room, and write how this gathering affected you emotionally. Don't wait—it is important that you do it now. This is deep soul work.

Woman Reborn

I am dazzled, dizzy,
spinning—spinning
from the winding sheet that knows no end—unfurled
from a silk sari, layer after
layer of shimmer, drifting,
mounding; mountains of
cream and celadon rise
toward my hips. Nowhere
is everywhere as the swiftly
swirling planet shifts beneath
my leaping feet. Dervishes
of gold spots glow like colliding
suns and I am one, many,
and all in the same
soaring moment.

—Therèse, March 31, 2007

Final Dialogue

Now, you are finished with this work. You have done what we have asked of you, and we are grateful and showering you with blessings. All will be as it is meant to be from here on, for you and for your family. Have no more fears. They are not worthy companions for you.

As I finished this book, and the CD, many difficulties arose in my physical being and my emotional life. If I am doing what is true and right for me, why is it so painful?

You have warned those who set foot on this path that it is not easy. Why should it be different for you who guide others? You must experience these things in order to teach them authentically. And have we not shown you that you are strong? Now, it is time to rest and prepare for what will come. Do not be surprised by anything.

I feel a warning.

No, not a warning; a preparation. Watch your choice of words! You now know the power of the guides in your life and the power of your own knowing. You are a being of great compassion. Others will return that to you. Your life is now beginning.

You mean my next life!

We mean your intentional life, the life that your earlier life prepared you for. We remind you to teach others. The time is critical. We cannot wait longer. See your planet and her suffering, and you know what is to be done. Each must do their soul's work to stop the darkness. It is too late for argument. Just remember our presence and remind others of the presence in their lives of guid-

ance and purpose. They know but they have forgotten, momentarily. Yours is a planet that drowns out the quiet voices. This must change. Call on us. But for now, rest is called for. We will come again when the time is right.

I will miss your guidance.

We are never gone—you have not gotten this clear in your mind yet, but your heart knows. If we don't speak to you, it only means we are supporting your energy and have nothing to tell you at the moment. Be in peace. All are chosen, and more are noticing. You are not here to make war but to be peace. The Promise is infallible—that which you create will be of your choice. All will happen as you desire, consciously or unconsciously. The Truth is that all are creators of their own reality. Those who have forgotten their Promise can remember. That is what this work is for.

Afterword

So what has been happening to me since I thought I finished this book? Challenges! Health challenges, money challenges, where to live challenges. Why? Because the teacher often needs to be reminded of the lessons she is teaching. I began to stress about how to get this book out into your hands, rather than trusting the Universe to see to it in its own inimitable fashion. I started worrying about where to live, because I've reached a certain age and suddenly the doctors are saying, "Well, when you reach that age..." instead of, "Let's see what we can do to address that." I worried that I wasn't seeing enough of my children and my grandchildren as I focused on my work. I worried that some of my children, or my partner, needed more energy than I was giving. I worried that the world needed my help! My worried thoughts snowballed like a dung beetle rolling downhill—what an interesting and mixed metaphor. I was totally outside of everything I had learned and was readying to pass on to you in this book and CD. No wonder my health was becoming more and more problematic. My thoughts were creating a vortex of negativity, a stew of "what if" propositions.

And as I worried about the future, I went back to Florida for Thanksgiving with the family, including my ex-husband and his girlfriend. Driving to Jacksonville with my daughter, I found my thoughts dwelling on past issues that I didn't want to repeat. We stopped for lunch, and I let her out in front while I went to park, not wanting to *waste time*! In that mode, I stepped out of my car in the parking lot, stepped up on a curb as I turned to lock my car, and fell—hard! I was going and coming simultaneously, and that vortex of exhaustion and inattention brought me down.

Stunned, on my hands and knees, my car keys impaled in my palm, I watched my blood pooling on the sidewalk around the contents of my purse in slow motion. Total disbelief and shock as people began to gather around me, their voices coming from someplace echoing and far off. I thought of my daughter who was in the restaurant, and would soon come around the corner and see me lying there. I pulled myself to a sitting position and found my head cradled against the ample tummy of a seventy-something man who was on his way to Disney World. He must have seen lots of John Wayne movies, because he was yelling for someone to bring a belt as he pressed his thumb against an artery in my wrist. His wife came running, bringing a towel from the kitchen to staunch the bleeding. "Let go of her! You're not a doctor!" she commanded, pressing the towel to my palm, keys and all. She was a retired nurse, but blanched at the sight of the keys buried in my hand, the automatic door lock dangling against my wrist.

The ambulance came. My blood pressure and sugar levels signaled "real" shock, and as my daughter stroked my head and I silently chanted my calming mantra of "Maui waterfall, Maui waterfall," they loaded me in and took me to the regional hospital.

Months later, I am still recovering from the soft tissue damage done to my leg and hip in that accident, and the continuing medical bills. My punctured hand, my sprained wrist, fingers, and shoulders, and my torqued neck are healed. My lower back, hip, and left knee are not. Further exploration revealed that the shock I experienced was multiplied by the memories in my cells of the day my son was struck down in the street and I knelt beside him on the concrete, the wail of the ambulance in my ears. The fall recreated the physical images and emotional memories buried deep in my body, as had the falling to my knees by his hospital bed so many years ago. Though I was disappointed in myself—oh yes, I have to admit that—I was able to look back this month and accept the confirmation I received of cellular memory and know that I would share this with my readers and workshop participants. I still had not acknowledged the implicit message in the going forward and backward at the time of my fall. The concern of my family about my health added more pressure to the "back and forthing" of my decision-making process. I was not off the hook yet, though I have been thinking a lot about Inanna!

My calendar was covered with notations for doctor follow-up on medications for the continuing blood pressure problems, a diagnosis of diabetes based on the blood sugar levels, and treatments for the muscle and tissue damage ranging from acupuncture to deep tissue massage. And in the midst of all this, the doctors determined, through a sleep test, that I was not getting enough oxygen at night because of sleep apnea. I began sleeping with a mask that forces air into my nose and keeps me breathing steadily through the night. Taken alone, none of these were enough to derail me from my wisdom. Together was another thing.

I continued to pray, meditate, and argue with myself over the same issues that were with me before the accident, and I began to write about the cellular information my body was revealing. Have you noticed that I was not following up on *my* Promise? The one where I was to teach about women's history, her challenges, and her beautiful spiritual life? Evidently my guides had noticed too, because in the midst of all of these issues which had only added to my financial problems, my family concerns, and my inner debate on where to live and do my work, my left eye was struck from within by flashes that resembled strobe lights and lightning racing around the retina. A strange veil appeared over my vision, and the ophthalmologist became my next best friend, another notation on my already filled medical calendar. Fortunately, my retina was intact, though I had experienced something called a Posterior Vitreous Detachment. Or as the nice doctor said, "As we age…"

This was a direct, no-nonsense message to me about what I was looking at. I had become a patient, not a person. My guidance had gotten fuzzy; I was peering into the darkness. And therein was my wake-up call. I have taught the importance of intuition, backed up by the emotional feelings of "good" and "bad," and I was too overwhelmed with negative thoughts to feel my feelings. I know that when I'm doing the right thing, my intuition sends me a good feeling. When I'm not in my right place, I get bad feelings, as in sad, stressed, or frustrated. In the worst-case scenario, the emotion is fear: fear that what is wanted won't appear, as in good health, good relationships, and good experiences. And yes, that old nemesis of not making others happy. Fear is all about lack and loss of faith, otherwise known as the Dark Night of the Soul. No matter how often I experienced or taught about it, there was some part of me that was still programmed in the old way of being.

I am happy to report that this malaise is lifting following the experience with my eye. My guidance has been here, sending me messages in every possible form. Thankfully, I finally saw! It was also a message to pass along to you. Finding our Promise, telling our Truth, and embarking on our Path will not guarantee a problem-free life. What they *will* guarantee is that when we are not in our True Promise, our guidance will notify us to pay attention. When we pay attention, we will experience a life that is free of *attachment* to problematic issues. We have the power to readjust our thinking to the perspective of possibilities.

Thoughts are energy, as we have learned, and will bring us what we focus on. I am removing my focus from lack and fear, once again, and am seeking partnership with success and joy. Every time I am challenged, it takes less energy to return me to center and to calm. Daily, before my altar, I visualize myself healthy, happy, and dancing! May you tune in to your inner wisdom and experience the joy of connection to right-being that has been promised to you. My greatest hope is that in living my life from a sense of joy and purpose, others will also see the possibilities in the challenges, and maybe won't be challenged as often or as severely as some of us have been. In reading the lives of spiritual teachers throughout history, I am so encouraged by their return, again and again, to right-being on their own particular path. No matter what detours and wrong exits I have taken, something holy brings me back to the path.

The soul calls upon us to return to that wisdom which we received about our Promise. This knowing comes from the same place and the same voices as the dialogues in Part Two and the last dialogue. You too have this knowing and this guidance, though your soul will present it differently than mine. Trust yourself. Trust your senses. Trust your wisdom. Trust your intuition. Most of all trust that the guidance you receive through your senses, your wisdom, and your intuition is meant to come to you and that it will reveal its purpose when you are ready. Finally, trust the process and your higher self, knowing that you can reprogram your subconscious, make peace with your ego, and connect with the God and Goddess within. The earth is ready now.

It seems to me that it is important to address a movement that has taken over the airways, the Internet, and soon the book world—the phenomenon known as *The Secret*. A local group invited us to a viewing of this movie in October of 2006. The buzz was already enormous as the Internet picked up on the availability of this *new and exciting* breakthrough in the power of attracting relationships and wealth. As a spiritual teacher, I am always interested in what others have to say about energy work, and looked forward to the evening. Ten minutes after the film began, I was ready to leave, a strange restlessness overtaking my body. The opening portion was mystical, referring to esoteric symbology, ancient rites, Masons, knights—all the things that grabbed our attention in the phenomenon known as *The Da Vinci Code*. But the exciting and adventurous beginning was only a teaser, an opening to the world of ministers, motivational speakers, and writers for such publications as *Chicken Soup for the Soul*, to tell us how they had become rich and famous. The age-old stories that first had their modern resurrection in the power of positive thinking movement had been repackaged for the fast-track generation.

My active detector for anything smacking of McSpirituality began buzzing. Even the words New Age have been problematic for me—everything spiritual is ancient, not new. Only the packaging and the "hook" are redesigned for today's audience. The same downside is still present. If you've been reading this book with intention, you already know what that is. Your Promise must come first. The power of the energetic universe and our thoughts *can* be harnessed to the procurement of goods, but our pact with our soul is so much larger than that. The first step is to determine what our soul desires in order to bring our fully flowered self into being. Then, using the skills and tools of energy and mind, we can build that life. That's what this book is about.

I sincerely believe that anything that helps focus us on the spiritual path can be a positive experience. However, when it becomes a cultural directive that Oprah and others in the mainstream media tout as the "fix" we have all been looking for, we know there is bound to be a downside. When I went to get my hair done in January, my hairdresser asked me if I'd seen *The Secret*. My e-mail content doubled with people asking me if I'd seen *The Secret*. Local radio interviewed everyone they could find to talk about *The Secret*. It signals to me that our culture is desperately seeking answers, and when a slickly packaged film says all you have to do is think it and it will be yours, we want to believe. There are now, several months later, many in the therapy field who are treating guilt-ridden patients because they aren't able to control their lives: those who are sick and believe they brought it upon themselves; those who are deserted by their mates and *know* if they had just believed harder it wouldn't have happened; those who didn't meet Bruce Springsteen even though they visualized it perfectly.

The dangers of presenting one-dimensional information where the purpose is to accumulate "stuff" is that we are only adding to the malaise our planet is feeling already. Anything that denies the necessity of facing the hard questions, dealing with emotional issues, family issues, and world issues from a spiritual perspective, denies the experience of the greatest teachers and saints who ever taught. Even Jesus asked that he be spared his final torment, but it was not to be. Is it because he didn't have the power to change what was about to happen? He yielded to a greater power—a choice that would introduce a gentle, kind, and loving way of life to the world. This was his Promise. *The Secret* leaves out service to humanity, honor to our ancestors, honor to our planet, and focuses on worship of the bigger house, the larger bank account, and the perks that come with fame.

Few of us would forgo the bigger bank account and a little more leisure in our lives. However, every minute of every day of our lives reflects our spiritual values. It is not always simple. Those who would begin to turn their eyes to their inner work from their focus on the accumulation of goods are not well served by a simplistic instruction book. Learning about how energy works is a wonderful thing, and I believe it will help us heal and attract those things into our lives that are loving and powerful. I also believe that the Universe is a multifaceted and multidimensional place with a lot of other forces at work, and if you place a picture on the bulletin board of the house of your dreams on the coast of California, and forty others place the same picture on their bulletin board, you won't all get it! Certainly *The Secret* has a message that can be used as a tool, but only one tool in a very big toolbox. Remember the poem by Rumi that says to welcome all into our house. Be open and thank those who point the way, but be true to what your heart tells you.

We are on a holy quest, serving the past, our present, and the future. If we deny the call, we have nothing to lose but the very soul of us—and we have staked our lives on this in the past.

I told Lance so many times as I was writing "I wish I could go with my book!" I was so dissatisfied with putting the meditations and visualizations on paper without the music and the emotion that comes out of my workshops. He suggested that I record a CD, which I did. When Michael Hoppé agreed to license his music to me so that it could accompany my voice on my CD, I knew another dimension was opening. His generosity and heart, obvious in his music, is truly who he is.

Lance offered *Heart and Soul Meditations* to complete the package. I am blessed beyond believing. Everything is open in this time of love and growth.

I bless, in advance, all those who find this book and all of those who encouraged me and read early drafts, especially Lance, who has edited all of my work, and my children, who are an endless resource of love both on and off the planet. There is no one with whom I would trade my life.

—Therèse
   March 14, 2007
   Oceanside, California

Appendix I

Timeline of Historical Truth for Women

FROM EARLY HISTORY TO THE PRESENT

I believe in the power and mystery of naming things.
Language has the capacity to transform our cells, rearrange
our learned patterns of behavior and redirect our thinking.
I believe in naming what's right in front of us because that
is often what is most invisible.

—Eve Ensler, writer *(The Good Body, The Vagina Monologues),*
Performer, and philanthropist

This appendix is not pleasant reading. If you believe as Eve does, and as I do, that the naming and looking at what is right in front of us is transformational, you will read on. The purpose is to explore the amount of difficult and painful material that is the genetic heritage of women, and that woman is currently experiencing on a global level. Only then will you be ready to remove these unacknowledged painful memories from your emotional body and move forward into your fullness and beauty as a woman, acknowledging those things that must be addressed from your position of strength.

221

When you read the information here—and it is certainly only a tiny part of history in a highly condensed form—you will understand why it is important to do the work of honoring your ancestors and those who share the planet with you now. Remember as you read that the purpose is not to upset or sadden you, but to encourage you to bring an equal balance to the history of women through your thoughts and actions. The emotions that arise in us, as historical and current facts are revealed, tend to be negative: anger, sadness, fear, helplessness, etc. Without understanding your history, the history passed down to you from the women in your mother's line and your father's line, you will hold the memory and pass it on to the next generation.

As I have mentioned several times, there is a great deal of science available that proves how past conditioning is stored in our subconscious and our cells. Books by cellular biologists Candace Pert and Bruce Lipton were helpful to me in understanding the process, while Deepak Chopra and Jean Houston's beautiful interpretations of quantum physics brought clarity to the spiritual aspects of science. Only in the knowing can we change our reactions, though we cannot change the actual past.

In Part Four there are exercises in revisiting the past, honoring and forgiving, and bringing strength and love into the women in our future. Doing the exercises reveals the strength and courage exhibited by women in the times that are darkest for them. Through them, we transform the negative emotions into admiration and love. When you reach an understanding, and do your work, you will not forget; but you will feel a lightness of being as you transfer the genetic memory from your cells to your feminine knowing and from there into action.

Damage that women are doing to themselves, and their daughters, right now will remind you that the work is not yet done where all humans are on an equal footing. Non-thinking, non-feeling individuals or organizations propagate old patterns. Thinking and feeling people are changing old patterns with compassion, love, and the will to make a difference. Wherever there is a negative, there are positive influences trying to right the balance. Think of this next section as an opportunity to see both where we are out of alignment with our Promise and Truth and where we are in alignment and can bring change.

When you have done some of the exercises, a dialogue with other women and real men in your life will result from your compassion and understanding of what being a woman has meant throughout history. From that platform, we carry forward our female history, honoring the past and looking actively in the present for women who are deserving of our praise and assistance, with an eye to the future women who are relying on us for our wisdom, not our youth.

The Timeline: Some facts

Women of the prehistoric times provided over 60 percent of the food for the family—meat was rare. The "age of the hunters" was actually the age of the gatherers. Though anthropologists found killing weapons more interesting, women invented sacks to transport the food they gathered, tools for digging, and slings for carrying their children. Besides nurturing the race inside themselves, they saved it from extinction, thus creating the honor and worship of women.

Women in 3800 BC were honored healers and priestesses. In Sumerian myth, Nammu is the maker of the world and doesn't have a male counterpart. The following words appear in the *Epic of Gilgamesh*, the earliest saga ever written, translated from clay tablets:

Inanna, Queen of Heaven and Earth, maiden, mother and crone.

A powerful role model, she is Goddess, protectress, sensuous female, and intelligent, powerful politician. She is aware, we are told in all the writings, of her position and obligation in the world. She is the great mediator. She is shown holding her breasts, the Mother of All, implying great fertility. Later she was also known as Ishtar.

A partnership model, based on worship of the goddess and equal recognition of the sexes, existed for thousands of years. We did not *begin* as male-dominated and warlike peoples.

The civilization that flourished in Old Europe between 6500 BC and in Crete until 1450 BC enjoyed a long period of uninterrupted peaceful living which produced artistic expressions of graceful beauty and refinement, demonstrating a higher quality of life than many androcratic, classed societies... (Marija Gimbutas, archaeologist, author of *The Civilization of the Goddess: The World of Old Europe*)

Sophia in Greek, *Hohkma* in Hebrew, *Sapientia* in Latin, all mean "wisdom." The Gnostic Christians believed Sophia was the mother of creation. Her symbol, the dove, represents spirit. She is crowned by stars, a Middle Eastern icon, to indicate her absolute divinity. Later Christians portrayed Mary, the Mother of God, with her feet on the earth (often on a snake) with a dove above her head, surrounded with stars.

Adam's first wife is acknowledged in the first book of Genesis as being created at the same time, from the earth. Not until later do we hear that Adam is "lonely" and Eve is brought forth from Adam's rib. What happened between "He created them both, male and female," to Adam's being lonely? Many things have been written about the fact that he had a first wife, named Lilith, in the writings of many religions, and that he complained that wife number one wasn't obedient; she refused to "lie beneath." Lilith, in a turn difficult even for those who were rewriting the Bible, became the symbol of evil. She, according to myth and legend, killed babies in their cribs. Up until recent times, certain sects put a mark on their children to protect them from Lilith. (Similarities to Medusa, also a child killer, are noted.)

The snake, the holiest of animal symbols for women—healing, change, wisdom—was also touched with the evil wand and began its descent into literature at man's hand. In the garden, the snake turned into Satan, and on Medusa's head, a symbol of woman's darkness. In spite of this, many goddess temples continued to use the snake in their ceremonies. The ability of the snake to shed its skin and regenerate was symbolic of the seasons and the human desire for change, growth, and in some cases, reincarnation.

While we are on the subject of the Bible, it is important to note the translations of the most famous prayer of Christianity—the Lord's Prayer. The Lord's Prayer in the Aramaic, "Abwoom de Bwushmaya," was altered to make it read "Our Father Who Art in Heaven." The correct translation, according to many Aramaic scholars, is a version of the following: "Oh Cosmic birther," or "Oh mother/father God." "Oh, birther of the Cosmos, focus your light within us," is the translation by Saadi Neil Douglas-Klotz.

A beautiful treatise by Julian of Norwich, a Christian Mystic in 1373, includes this line: "As truly as God is our father, so truly is God our mother."

As the attempts to change the matriarchy or the partnership model to a patriarchal model increased, Greek and Roman goddesses were often altered to have lineage from their father rather than mother

Example: The tale of Athena springing from the temple (forehead) of her father Zeus. According to mythology, Zeus marries his sister and divides the world with his brothers. Scholars have discovered that Hera, his wife, was the primary goddess of the time and Zeus got his power by marrying her. The earliest and greatest Greek monuments are to Hera. Since her name is not Greek, she pre-dates the Greek pantheon. In order to diminish her, she is transformed in later writing into a shrewish scolding jealous wife.

Zeus lay with Metis, his other wife, and then had a dream that the child would be more powerful than he, so he turned Metis into a fly and swallowed her. Metis had already planned for the eventuality, and arranged for Zeus to be cleaved through the forehead, whereupon Athena sprang from his head. He, of course, survived and the tale became that he had managed to procreate without help of a female.

Ge or Gaia is the main goddess until the powers of procreation shift from female to male through this myth. Once Athena is born from the head of Zeus, she and the furies become staunch supporters of everything masculine.

Writers of this time were centered on changing the way of things to a male-centric belief system

Example: In Aeschylus' *Eumenides*, Orestes is pursued by the furies for killing his mother. In the climax, the Sun God, Apollo, announces: "The mother is not the parent of that which is called her child; but only nurse of the newly planted seed that grows. *The parent is he who mounts.*" Orestes is then saved by Athena who says Apollo is correct in his judgment that the father is the true parent of the child, the mother merely the nurse. Therefore the murder of any woman is not as serious as the murder of a man (or wife/husband).

And yet, did you know that Pythagoras, Socrates, and Plato all had female teachers? They were, in order, Aristoclea, Diotima, and Aspatia.

Example: Phoebe has given her dwelling place to Apollo—therefore in the Greek plays, the woman is more powerful but finds good in giving her power to the man.

This change to *giving away* replaced a matriarchal society where men went to live with the woman's family and assumed her family name. In many Middle Eastern cultures, a man had to simply say, "I refuse to take your cattle to pasture" and he was divorced. This is obvious recognition of the fact that the woman owned the property and the man had joined *her* family.

Examples of implied or direct prejudice

Plutarch says "You must keep her on a tight rein…Women want total freedom, or rather total license. If you allow them to achieve complete equality with men, do you think they will be any easier to live with? Not at all. Once they have achieved equality, they will be your masters."

When the Knight finds the Grail or other holy object, he opens it and the world is healed. When Pandora opens the box, she releases chaos on the world—she is nosy.

Cassandra was a servant of the goddess and a prophet and seer of world renown. When she prophesied the truth of what would happen in the Trojan War, she became a traitor and was ostracized. Now, when someone gives a warning, or tries to say we should look at something more closely, they are accused of being a Cassandra, or a wet blanket.

Misogyny taken to the extreme

Hypatia was known as the great philosopher and mathematician of the glorious age of Alexandria. Letters sent to "The Philosopher," with no other address, arrived at her door. She was dragged from her classroom and brutally murdered by Christians who feared a learned woman—she was flayed with oyster shells. Before long, the great brain trust of Alexandria had migrated elsewhere out of fear of persecution, and the golden age of Egypt came to an end.

The inquisition/witch hunts killed over one million people—some say four million and others as many as nine million. Entire villages were destroyed to root out women who were healers.

I can't imagine that they didn't *know* exactly how many were murdered, but having seen the devastation of war, hurricanes, and tsunamis, I now understand a body count is not always done. The last witch hunts occurred in Massachusetts, our very own bastion of the proper and the learned. The main cause for being accused was that a woman could heal. If the doctors and priests couldn't, then you must be a witch if you could.

Robert Johnson, a famous student of Jung, gives a couple of throw-away lines to the Inquisition and the witch hunts in his book *Men* when he says that women were burned at the stake who were "odd."

The only remnants of this murderous time are witches on broomsticks at Halloween—ugly women with warts on their long noses. Why do we not study the extent of this holocaust in school?

Equality when?

The great religions are all founded on the idea that women are inferior to men, and they grow stronger over time. Example: "Blessed art Thou, O Lord our God, King of the Universe, that Thou hast not made me a woman," a daily prayer of Hebrew males. Countries that have their religious books as part of their judicial system today—Pakistan and Israel, for example—give heavier weight to the rights of males.

Example: Under *Sharia* law a woman's word in a court of law is worth half of a man's. Under *Rabbinical* law a woman has no right to institute divorce, while a man does.

Christian women still fight for the right to the pulpit. Women of several Orthodox sects are not allowed in the church after childbirth until they stop bleeding. A woman I know missed the Baptism of her own daughter because she was considered too "unclean" to enter the church.

And yet Jesus taught equality of all, and he welcomed women in his ministry. Early Christian groups were supported and organized by a majority of women. Mary Magdalene was his most trusted apostle—a woman of high family who supported his ministry. Somehow, through the magic of revisionist thinking, Pope Gregory I (ca. 540–604) turned her into a prostitute. This pronouncement conveniently eliminated her as a mystical teacher and was memorialized in our own time in both movies and musicals on Broadway.

Joan of Arc was burned at the stake for impersonating a man, an accusation against her that was equal to treason.

Bright and ambitious women throughout the last centuries had to dress as men to study, write, and be taken seriously.

Women who fought for the vote in the United States, in the early twentieth century, were imprisoned and had their children taken from them. Sometimes they were called mentally deficient. When people saw the special *Iron Jawed Angels* on television, they were amazed that this had happened in the U.S. in such recent times. What kind of footnote did suffragettes receive in high school history books?

Upper class women of the Victorian Age took poison (arsenic) daily to keep their fair skin and lethargy intact. It was just before this that men convinced Western women to give birth with their legs in the air! Why we acquiesced is another book altogether.

At the women's rights convention in 1851, a well-meaning upper class man suggested that women shouldn't need rights since men were their protectors. This was the response from one woman.

Sojourner Truth: 1851 at a women's rights convention

That man over there says women need to be helped into carriages and lifted over ditches, and to have the best place everywhere. Nobody ever helps me into carriages or over puddles, or gives me the best place—and ain't I a woman?
Look at this arm! I have ploughed and planted and gathered into barns, and no man could head me—and ain't I a woman?
I could work as much and eat as much as a man—when I could get it—and bear the lash as well. And ain't I a woman?
I have borne thirteen children and seen most of 'em sold off to slavery, and when I cried out with my mother's grief, none but Jesus heard me—and ain't I a woman?

In case we insist this is old news

From chastity belts to bourkas, testimony is given to man's fear of woman's sexuality. What is it they fear? In Afghanistan, women's lives hang in the balance if they read or try to teach other women. But we're not just talking Afghanistan, Iran or Iraq. In 2005 in Carlsbad, California, I saw a brand new SUV with a bumper sticker: "I Beat Women." This would be against the law if it was a minority that was named. His other bumper sticker? "I don't give a fuck if you're offended."

I *am* offended. When this type of person doesn't feel comfortable with that attitude, I will cease to be offended.

Laura Bush, the wife of the president, was asked by Barbara Walters what she would concentrate on in her husband's second term. She replied: "Boys, because girls and women have received all the attention." With respect, there is some attention we would like to avoid, as in the following examples of current-time issues.

Just across the border from El Paso, in Mrs. Bush's home state of Texas, there is an infamous town named Juarez. In this town, over 368 women and girls have been killed or disappeared in the past decade. Many were raped, mutilated, and tortured, including a six-year-old girl. According to VDay.org, "The situation is dire for women in Juarez who already struggle under great adversity working in globalized factories—mainly American owned and with exports to the U.S.—for $4.00 a day." See the web site for details on how women are mobilizing to bring this horror to the eyes of the press.

In the UN report titled *Ending Violence Against Women* released in France in October, 2006, the conclusion was that "violence against women is severe and pervasive" worldwide, with one in three women subjected to intimate partner abuse during her lifetime. "Murders of women often involve sexual violence, with between forty and seventy percent of women murdered being killed by their husbands or boyfriends in Australia, Canada, Israel, South Africa and the United States." The report noted that more than 130 million girls are victims of female genital mutilation. Female infanticide, prenatal sex selection, and systematic neglect of girls were said to be widespread in South Asia, Southeast Asia, North Africa, and the Middle East.

In the September 20, 2006 issue of *The Reader*, a widely consulted weekly for San Diegans searching out movies, restaurants, and local go-ings-on, the cover story was "The Hip List: You Had To Be There, Own It, Wear it, Hear It." On the "best" list, they named SIK World Produc-tions, a company that makes T-shirts for infants that read, in part, "My daddy's a motherfucker," "Satan, Jr.," "Nice tits, can I try one?" The ones for men and women were even more insulting, but infants and children as pornographic billboards is stretching the limit, even in today's climate of anything goes. When we are talking about honoring and peace, it is hard to understand why a widely circulated San Diego weekly rewards this kind of perversion.

The top two causes of death in girls ages ten to nineteen, worldwide, are AIDS and pregnancy.

In 1996, India finally passed a law to ban sex determination tests which were being used to abort girls. In 2006, ten years later, only one conviction has been obtained and over four *million* girls have been aborted.

Genital mutilation, perpetrated on young girls in diverse cultures the world over, is not being eradicated, yet. Doctors in New York have been known to do this procedure on children of U.N. representatives. Their reasoning? It's not up to us to tell people how to practice their cultural mores. What if they practiced cannibalism? Would we set up restaurants to accommodate their "cultural mores?" As usual, it is up to women to make a change. Until the mothers and aunties of these young girls are willing to stop the cycle of disfiguring violence, it won't happen. Eve Ensler—www.Vday.org—and her organization are doing phenom-enal grass roots work, and so is C.A.R.E. For me, it boggles the mind that this "other-inflicted" torture goes on as women in America choose a treatment I've just become aware of—labiaplasty. Read on.

In her book *Beauty Junkies*, *New York Times* reporter Alex Kuczyn-ski tells us about the $15-billion industry that is known as "cosmetic enhancement." In an interview with *Publishers Weekly* in July, 2006, Ms. Kuczynski, who has undergone some minor surgeries and Botox herself, is asked, "What are some of the grossest things you've seen people do in the name of beauty?"

Her reply: "I was disturbed by labiaplasty, a procedure where the inner genitals of women are tightened and the outer labia cleaned up, like we're all supposed to look like porn actresses. It makes you wonder if they'll ever feel comfortable riding a bike again. I've seen people who have gone through 12 different procedures to remove excess skin from their bodies after losing dramatic amounts of weight with gastric bypass surgery. They're like dripping wax figures."

Educated and loving women go to house parties where they receive treatments to remove laugh lines from their faces. Without discussing the loss of the "map of life" written on the face, we need to acknowledge the true danger that resides in surgery and injections of foreign bodies into our bodies. The pretty pictures on the brochures are not what you see behind closed doors in hospitals and doctors' suites. These procedures were invented to help those who were disfigured in a natural way or through body trauma. They are not on the same level as Tupperware.

On September 7, 2006, a beautiful twenty-four-year-old named Fabiola DePaula died in Massachusetts after giving $3300.00 to an un-licensed doctor for a nose job and liposuction. These operations were performed on a massage table in the basement of a condominium, a place known to the community as an operating theatre for anyone who wanted to be more beautiful. "There should be a lesson learned from the death of this young woman," the district attorney said. "People think this is an extension of getting my nails done, getting my hair done." Her friend said the sad thing is that Paula had no need for the surgery. "She was absolutely gorgeous, not only on the outside but on the in-side." What drove her to this place? Sociologists say it's because she was Brazilian, and the women of Brazil are known to go under the knife to achieve the beauty for which their nation is famous.

I think it is a world-wide phenomenon of women reverting to the beauty equals value thinking. Susan Sarandon, a beautiful woman inside and out, said the surgery alternative would cause her to look like a "fe-male impersonator version of myself."

In *Inventing the Rest of our Lives,* author Suzanne Braun Levine acknowledges having *a one-time procedure of removing the puffy bags under my eyes, and I am happy with the result; I feel that my less tired-looking face is more expressive of my well-being.* But she separates this from the idea of getting injections or liposuction or surgeries that would mean *watching myself age over and over again in between*. She also decries the medical establishment's assumption that women are *small men*. In other words, all medical research done on men can be extrapolated to fit women, just in a smaller way. We now know that is false and dangerous.

And lastly, the idiocy goes on. In February, 2007, a headline on a UK site said, "No vaginas please, we're Floridian." A theatre near Jacksonville, Florida, was part of the great volunteer effort to show "The Vagina Monologues," a play that has raised more than 40 million dollars to fight violence against women. A woman complained that she was passing the theatre and her niece asked her what a vagina was. Her embarrassment was so acute, she threatened to call the police. The theatre, which had a contract with Eve Ensler that specifically mandated the word vagina, since that was the whole point, changed the marquee to read "The Hoo-hah Monologues." We have a long way to go.

Please read the next article for a good reason to smile on the women in your life.

Why We Need Women Friends

*Every friend represents a world in us, a world possibly
not born until they arrive,
and it is only by this meeting that a new world is born.*

—Anais Nin, writer

In early 2000, a UCLA study on the effects of friendship on women was released (Taylor et al., "Biobehavioral responses to stress in females," *Psychological Review*, July vol.). An article by Gale Berkowitz highlighted some of the findings of the study.

1) Friendships between women are special.

2) Scientists show that in addition to helping us remember who we really are and filling the emotional gaps in our relationships, friendship between women can counteract stress.

3) Studies on male stress do NOT apply to women. Fight or flight, the standard opinion about stress, does not happen with women. Stress for men releases a cascade of hormones that initiates fight or flight. In women, there is a larger behavioral repertoire. The hormone oxytocin is released in women, buffering any fight or flight and encouraging her to

bond with other women and children. When she actually engages in this "tend and befriend" behavior, more oxytocin is released, which further calms and counters stress.

4) Two female scientists began the research when they noted that stress in the lab sent the men into their offices to close the door and sent the women into straightening up the lab and talking about the stress with other women. (They didn't just choose between picking up a spear or running away!) Drs Klein and Taylor discovered that by not including women in stress research, scientists had made a huge mistake. The fact that women respond to stress differently than men has huge implications for our health.

5) When women are too busy in their lives, the first thing they jettison is the thing they need most—women's friendships. That's a major error. Friends are healing.

Reconnect or begin to connect with women in twos or groups. It will be one of the most healing things you will do for your health and happiness. If the men or children in your life are threatened by this, remind them gently of their bonding around sports, clubs, friends, and fraternity. This is your support group. I believe that the improved health enjoyed by those who belong to religious groups are more about society than faith, though faith is important. The community church, synagogue, mosque, or women's club all calm the outsider fear of the lone human. Add to this a connection with like-minded women and you will feel the joy of the tribe. As the wonderful poet, Mary Oliver, says in the last four lines of her beautiful poem "The Summer Day":

> "Tell me, what else should I have done?
> Doesn't everything die at last, and too soon?
> Tell me, what is it you plan to do
> with your one wild and precious life?"

Appendix II

Recommended Books and Sources

- *Insecure at Last by* Eve Ensler
- *The Vagina Monologues* by Eve Ensler
- *New and Selected Poems* by Mary Oliver
- *West Wind: Poems and Prose Poems* by Mary Oliver
- *Quantum Healing* & *The Book of Secrets* by Deepak Chopra
- *A Natural History of the Senses* by Diane Ackerman
- *At the Root of this Longing* by Carol Lee Flinders
- *A Woman's Journey to God* by Joan Borysenko, PhD
- *Woman: An Intimate Geography* by Natalie Angier
- *The Enlightened Heart* by Stephen Mitchell
- *The Search for the Beloved* & *A Mythic Life* by Jean Houston, PhD
- *The Feminine Face of God* by Sherry Ruth Anderson & Patricia Hopkins
- *Parallel Worlds* by Michio Kaku
- *Restoring the Goddess* by Barbara G. Walker

- *The Crone* by Barbara G. Walker
- *Revelations of Women Mystics* by José de Vinck
- *A Short History of Myth* by Karen Armstrong
- *The Spiral Staircase* by Karen Armstrong
- *Signs of Life* by Angeles Arrien, PhD
- *The Four-Fold Way* by Angeles Arrien, PhD
- *Who Cooked the Last Supper?* by Rosalind Miles
- *Women of Wisdom* by Paula Marvelly
- *If Women Ruled the World*, edited by Sheila Ellison
- *Inventing the Rest of Our Lives* by Susan Braun Levine
- *The Hero Within* by Carol S. Pearson, PhD
- *Backlash* by Susan Faludi
- *Goddesses in Everywoman* by Jean Shinoda Bolen, MD
- *Molecules of Emotion* by Candace Pert, PhD
- *The Lost Daughters of China* by Karin Evans
- *Inanna: Queen of Heaven and Earth*, translated by Diane Wolkstein & Samuel Noah Kramer
- *Story of My Life* by George Sand
- *George Sand,* biography by Elizabeth Harlan
- *The Biology of Belief* by Bruce Lipton, PhD
- *Women's Ways of Knowing* by Mary Field Belenky, Blythe McVicker Clinchy, Nancy Rule Goldberger & Jill Mattuck Tarule
- *Where Two Worlds Touch* by Gloria D. Karpinski
- *Myths to Live By* by Joseph Campbell
- *The Majority Finds Its Past* by Gerda Lerner

- *Spinning Straw Into Gold* by Joan Gould
- *The Mists of Avalon* by Marion Zimmer Bradley
- *The Civilization of the Goddess* by Marija Gimbutas
- *Beauty Junkies* by Alex Kuczynski

Sources:
Angeles Arrien, PhD: *Preferential Shapes Test* & *Tarot Handbook*
Doreen Virtue, PhD: *Archangel Oracle Cards*

Recommended Music for Meditation, Visualization, and Ritual

- *Solace* by Michael Hoppé (Evocative and heartfelt music used on my CD *The Promise.*)

- *Requiem* by Michael Hoppé (Excellent for grief work)

- *Heart and Soul Meditations*, produced by Lance Ware (Instrumental version for meditation, guided version for sleep—also used on my CD *The Promise.*)

- *Alleluia & Kyrie* by Robert Gass (Meditative)

- *The Sacred Well: The Best of 2002* by 2002 (Meditative)

- *Land of Forever* by 2002

- *Shamanic Dream* by Anugama (Aboriginal music good for Sacred Feminine Visualization and Time Dimension Therapy)

- *She Carries Me* by Jennifer Berezan (Perfect for workshop ritual—includes Olympia Dukakis reading the Prayer of the Goddess)

- *Desires* by Chris Spheeris (For quiet times)

- *Musical Healing* by various artists (Especially number 10 for visualizations)

- *Songs of the Spirit* by Karen Drucker (Wonderful vocals to address specific issues)
- *Sacred Spirit I and II* from Higher Octave Music (Native American chants & dances)
- *Beloved* by Karen Drucker (Vocals—I use these for workshops)
- *The Promise* by Tim Janis (Great to use with ritual—very big scope)
- *State of Grace II* by Paul Schwartz (Some vocals—creates state of peace)
- *Chariots of Fire* by Vangelis (Rousing)

I highly recommend any classical music you find heart touching for ritual or visualization. In my case, it would be Rachmaninoff, Vivaldi, and Tchaikovsky to start. Chopin has many soft, contemplative pieces for quieter meditation. Vangelis has several pieces I would recommend also, though most are very stirring and are more suited to visualizations like the meadow.

Appendix III

The Search for the Grail Stories

The stories of adventure and the search for the Grail are written in a way that appeals to men, from the ancient Babylonian *Epic of Gilgamesh* to King Arthur and then Robin Hood. It is rare—actually, almost unheard of—for women to have been exposed to Grail stories from the female point of view. The reason is fairly simple: a woman's search has often been interior and circular, and women weren't in charge of what was put in the canon of high school and university literature. Only those few intrepid women who ranged beyond the required studies, or studied foreign cultures, tripped over the rich, mystical writings about women's journeys. And yet, myth helps us to make sense of our lives. How can women make sense of their lives, except as secondary players, when limited to men's stories?

From the beginning of recorded time, the Paleolithic period of 20,000 to 8000 BCE, humans saw themselves as separated from their spirituality. They painted, danced, and sang about their attempts to recover from that separation and enter into unity. The sky and nature represented the spiritual.

In the Neolithic, 8000 to 4000 BCE, humans became planters and harvesters and recognized the Great Mother as the earth herself, bringing about myths and stories that reflected the seasons. The onset of agricultural society was optimistic. People knew they would die, but they saw evidence for rebirth in the seed that became a plant. Most of us learned the story of Demeter and Persephone, which ended in the daughter spending part of the time in the underworld. Demeter, the mother, caused the land to go fallow during the time her daughter was gone: a visible sign of mourning. But when Persephone arose from the underworld, everything bloomed.

We learn that this was a satisfactory explanation of the growing season, but in our *enlightened* times, most of us miss the human message contained in the story: we must be fallow at least part of the time; dream, search our inner selves, be aware of those things that are not green and growing; make time for mourning. Also, we must be aware of death, not cover it over. The ritual of death is controlled and antiseptic in our culture, including medicating, or even committing, those who show their grief in unacceptable ways. In other cultures, ashes on the head, keening, wailing as the body is carried through town or village, are all visible signs of loss and sadness. Those who mourn recover more quickly. No wonder there is an epidemic of depression as we store emotions in our body, waiting to discover them later.

The ancient story of Inanna, the most honored and first recorded goddess of the Sumerians, had a more painful message: we must actually die to ourselves *during life* in order to be born again. (Other cultures called Inanna Ishtar or Astarte, and Dumuzi becomes the earlier Adonis.) For a more familiar concept, think of the later story of the crucified and resurrected Christ.

The Story of Inanna

In the beginning, Inanna is having a dream life. The sensual story of her relationship with her lover Dumuzi predates the Song of Solomon, its gorgeous prose in praise of bodily and human love unsurpassed in the thousands of years since. But, as happens in story, Inanna decided to leave paradise and go to the underworld, ruled by her sister.

> *From the Great Above she opened her ear to the Great Below.*
> *From the Great Above, the goddess opened her ear to the Great Below.*
> *From the Great Above, Inanna opened her ear to the Great Below.*
> *My Lady abandoned heaven and earth to descend to the underworld.*
> *Inanna abandoned heaven and earth to descend to the underworld.*
> *She abandoned her office of holy priestess to descend to the underworld.*

And so begins the middle section of the myth of Inanna titled "Inanna: Queen of Heaven and Earth" as translated by Diane Wolkstein and Samuel Noah Kramer. I will tell the rest of this story in my own words.

In the middle of her life, savoring the sweet love of her husband Dumuzi and the honor of her people, Inanna was called to visit her sister, Ereshkigal, Queen of the Underworld, who was mourning the death of her husband. Ereshkigal was also about to give birth. (Some say Ereshkigal was Inanna's twin, or the dark part of her own soul.)

Before she set out, she put on all of her power ornaments, including the shugurra, *the crown of the steppe, on her head. She tied lapis around her neck, wrapped her royal robes around her body, bound the breastplate of power over her, put the gold ring on her wrist, and carried the lapis measuring rod and line in her hand. Inanna left her loyal servant, Ninshubur, at the gate. All of these are symbolic of the gifts we have in life: communication, love, friendship, compassion, creativity, and wisdom. "If I do not return, set up a lament for me," Inanna instructed Ninshubur.*

She was prepared for all possibilities…but one. As she was ushered through the entrance and down into the underworld, she was stripped, at each of the seven levels, one by one, of not only her power ornaments but also her royal robes. She entered the presence of her dark sister totally nude and defenseless. Inanna is left to depend on her friend at the gate in the upper world. She herself is powerless.

When she arrived in the throne room, she was pronounced guilty by the judges of the underworld and Ereshkigal struck her down. She could see no good reason why Inanna had come to this place, except that she might want Ereshkigal's power. Inanna was a corpse, and was hung from a hook on the wall.

When Inanna did not return after three days and three nights, Ninshubur went from place to place seeking help. All responded, "She who goes to the dark city, stays there." Finally, Ninshubur went to Eridu to the temple of Enki, father of Inanna. He was greatly grieved and created two small beings, the size of flies. To one he gave the water of life, to the other the food of life. He told them to go to the underworld, sneak through the cracks, and when they got to the throne room they were to show compassion to the Queen of the Underworld, who was unattended in the birth of her child. He told them to respond, to mirror, each of her cries.

When she cries, "Oh! Oh! My insides!" cry also, "Oh! Oh! Your insides!" And so they did. As Ereshkigal continued her labor, the two small beings responded to each cry as they were instructed. "Oh! Oh! My belly!" Ereshkigal cried. "Oh! Oh! Your Belly," they cried in return, echoing her pain. Ereshkigal was seen and heard. She sighed: "Ah! Ah! My heart!" They sighed: "Ah! Ah! Your heart."

Ereshkigal, so touched by this compassion and recognition of her suffering, offered them any gift they would like. They asked for the corpse on the wall.

The corpse was given and they sprinkled the food of life on the corpse and the water of life on the corpse. And Inanna arose.

However, there was, as there always is, a catch. No one is allowed to leave the underworld without sending a replacement. When Inanna left, the demons of the underworld went with her to round up her replacement. They were fierce, frightening, and contained not one speck of compassion. They asked for Ninshubur, as they saw her awaiting at the gate, but Inanna would not give up her faithful servant and friend. They asked for her sons, who were in mourning dress of sackcloth for their mother, and fell at her feet when they saw her. She refused, saying her sons were loyal and loving.

Finally, in Uruk, by the big apple tree, Inanna found her beloved husband sitting on her throne dressed in splendid garments and wearing the gifts stolen from her on the way to the underworld. She pronounced him dead to her, the same words Ereshkigal had used to Inanna. The demons took Dumuzi. He pleaded with the god of justice for help. The god had mercy on him and changed him into a snake so he could escape. But he was finally caught, and in despair, called upon Inanna and his sister. Inanna took pity on him and allowed him to spend six months in the underworld; the other six months he was replaced by his sister. Thus the people had Dumuzi, the shepherd, the symbol of sweet grass, and the lord of all things that grew, for only six months of the year instead of twelve. When he returned from the underworld and reunited with his lover, Inanna, all was well. But now the people knew that death was a part of life.

Other than a good story to explain the earth being fertile six months and fallow for the other six, what else is in this story? First, the gifted one will not live a perfect life, in spite of her gifts. Even a goddess has to go into the darkness of the underworld to see clearly. Using your gifts will lead to challenges and struggles. Going inside, meeting your darkness and confronting your own ego, stripped of your usual gifts and/or defenses, is part of the process of growth. Secondly, mirroring one's own self, forgiving all of those ignored dark parts of us, will create an inner world that is habitable even by those we have blamed. Even Ereshkigal responded to kindness. Even Inanna gave Dumuzi some choices! Love as forgiveness is a major theme of the story, as Inanna welcomes Dumuzi back to the marriage bed when he returns from the underworld. Third, the people received the knowledge that nothing protects one from death:

even the goddess, with all her powers, was struck down. Also, the goddess who brings life also brings death. Every day is the death of who we were yesterday, but also the promise of who we will be tomorrow.

Resurrection through change is a strand that now enters myth, including Eastern and Western stories like Persephone's and Inanna's. Finally, accepting all that we have—our gifts—and all that we hide—our darker side—results in a full human existence. It *is* frightening to face our demons, but we will discover ourselves when we do. Then, when we return to the upper world of our everyday life, we will know our strength, our power, and our humanness. And, with blessing, we will no longer fear death. This is the true Grail—the cup of life.

The Grail Castle/The Fisher King

The legend of Gilgamesh, the stories of the Bible, and most subsequent stories rely on the external search for the power contained in man and the Grail. God was no longer trustworthy and had become a deity to be feared, or he had removed himself from human affairs. By going through rites of passage outside himself, as in the Arthurian legends and the time of the knights, the reward was found through sacrifice and suffering, and the warrior became pleasing to God. We see this even today as we name acts of war *heroic*, no matter what the cause, and certain acts of sacrifice foolish and unnecessary.

The following is a short synopsis of a traditional Grail story, called in French the *san greal*, or Holy Grail. Through arrangement of the letter *g*, *san greal* came to mean "True Blood." Thus Christianity entered into the picture in later versions. The Fisher King is the shortened story.

When Parsifal—the Holy fool—otherwise known as Perceval, sets off on his quest, he actually enters the Grail Castle and sees the wounded Fisher King. In his timidity, he fails to ask the question that will reveal the cause of the wound, and has to wander and suffer for years. The question he was meant to ask is, "Who does the Grail serve?" He has listened to others who tell him how to behave. He has listened to his limitations, as they were presented to him, and lost his opportunity to ask the question. So he must wander and suffer until he earns another opportunity to ask the question.

251

(So far, this sounds logical and reasonable, and we can find an easy moral in the story: if you are not true to yourself and listen to others, you will wander in the desert of incompletion.)

The wound of the King, however, has caused the land to dry up, the livestock to die, and the people to starve. Parsifal is a knight and should not fall victim to human frailty. Wounding has made the Fisher King impotent, thus causing the land, the livestock, and the people in the kingdom to be barren also. He could do nothing but fish, and it was at the lake that he would meet the knight who would come to the castle and neglect to ask the one question that would heal it all. Who does the Grail serve? Eventually, Parsifal, or Lancelot, solved the riddle and became the keeper of the Grail and the successor of the King. The Grail, and the lance used to wound the King, vanished when Parsifal died.

As time passed, the story morphed into another Christian quest story. In a later story, Lancelot's son, Galahad, became the true Grail knight, recovering the chalice from the Last Supper, and possibly the lance used by the Roman soldier to pierce the heart of the dying Jesus.

Some could read these earlier stories as comment on modern day leadership, but since the first story by Chrétien de Troyes was unfinished, all guesses as to the author's meaning are only guesses. For myself, as a woman reading this story, my strong intuition is that this was a warning. The whole society was set up around war: the Fisher King was wounded by a lance in a land dedicated to knightly activities. To me, the wounded land reflected the loss of the feminine side of humankind, including compassion, kindness, gentleness, love, and peace. As long as this part of the story was missing, the land and the people would suffer.

When I heard the instructions that I was to study the time when the Grail replaced the cauldron, I had no idea where that would take me. What I found would fill another book. The Grail stories are based on ancient Celtic stories of the magic cauldron of rebirth—a priceless object. The cauldron is symbolic of the feminine in various myths. The cauldron disappears—as the ancient rituals of women disappear—and becomes the property of man. Eventually, we have the Witches of Endor in Shakespeare's writing as a pale imitation of the true value of the cauldron and the female healers of olden times.

The failure of the knights was that they looked outside for the answer. The answer, the quest itself, lies inside. It was a wonderful day for me when I had the insight that *the wound of the Fisher King was the loss of the feminine.* When this insight was followed by my son Michael's message that the wound I carried was a portal, not a wound, I knew that woman's quest was altogether different than that we had been reading about for years. Letting go, trusting our voices, and following our guidance is what is required.

The Grail serves each of us. It bubbles up inside, washes us with the waters of peace and harmony, and restores us to our true meaning. The Grail—the cauldron—is our individual soul. In a woman, that soul is calling us to acknowledge the truth and power of our femaleness and make peace with the past history of the shunning punishment of women. What magnificence will shine on our planet when that is done! Whatever you have discovered to be your Promise, it will serve the purpose of balancing our beautiful planet in its own way. We are walking with you in Truth and Love, supported by the Promise made to us: we will have whatever we need to accomplish our soul's purpose.

End

Photo by Michael Myatt

About the Author

Therèse is a mother, grandmother, Somatic Intuitive Practitioner, Time Dimension Therapist, hypnotherapist, and co-director of ISIS: Institute for Sacred Integrative Somatherapies. She is the author of *A Time to Reap*, a novel; *Walking Your Walk: A Woman's Guide to a Spirit-Filled Life; Night Gardening: Passionate Poems for the Beloved*, with her partner Lance; and *Lot's Wife*, a chapbook of poems. Her work has been published in many books and literary magazines, including the Grammy-nominated *Grow Old Along With Me: The Best is Yet to Be*, where her work was read by Alfre Woodard. She lives in Oceanside, California, and Indian Shores, Florida. You can reach her at

www.IsisInstitute.org or Ttappouni@aol.com

Previous Work by Therèse Tappouni

- *Lot's Wife*, a chapbook of poetry
- *Walking Your Walk: A Woman's Guide to a Spirit Filled Life*
- *Night Gardening: Passionate Poems for the Beloved*, with her partner Lance Ware
- *A Time to Reap*, a novel

Anthologies

- *Grow Old Along With Me: The Best is Yet to Be*
- *Through a Child's Eyes: Poems and Stories about War*
- *Excalibur*